IKEBANA

IKEBANA

A FRESH LOOK
AT JAPANESE FLOWER ARRANGING

Diane Norman & Michelle Cornell

RIZZOLI NEW YORK

First published in the United States of America in 2002 by

RIZZOLI INTERNATIONAL PUBLICATIONS, INC.

300 Park Avenue South

New York, NY 10010

ISBN 0-8478-2494-2

First published in the United Kingdom in 2002 by Conran Octopus Limited

Publishing Director: Lorraine Dickey
Senior Editor: Katey Day
Project Editor: Sharon Amos

Creative Director: Leslie Harrington
Creative Manager: Lucy Gowans
Designer: Sue Storey

Photographer: Verity Welstead
Stylist: Miranda Swallow
Picture Research Manager: Liz Boyd
Picture Research: Marissa Keating

Production Manager: Adam Smith

Printed in China

Contents

What is ikebana?

Ikebana is an ancient art using flowers and plant material. It springs from a respect for nature deeply embedded within the Japanese culture. Like many other Japanese art forms, such as calligraphy, the tea ceremony and haiku poetry, ikebana is a discipline based on a fundamental way of living – a *do* or philosophy.

In the West, ikebana has sometimes been wrongly categorized as merely flower arranging, but doing so misses out on the subtlety, richness and depth of this ancient discipline. Through the arrangements we create, ikebana strengthens our connection with nature, is a powerful means of self-expression and develops our ability to see in new ways.

Ikebana is better translated as 'living flowers' or 'making flowers come alive'. The word itself can be separated into two parts, *ike* and *hana*: *hana* or *bana* means 'flower' or 'plant'; *ike* comes from three verbs, *ikeru*, *ikiru* and *ikasu*. Respectively, these mean 'to place or arrange plants', 'to live' and 'to make life clearer'. When the Japanese refer to the art of using flowers, they often simply say *Ohana*. In Japanese, adding the letter O to a word conveys a feeling of respect and, in this case, indicates a special attitude to flowers.

The relationship that the Japanese have with nature is more than just sentimental appreciation. Nature and spirit, life and art are not felt to be separate; the spirit of all life is present in the living beauty of nature. As you will see, the Japanese take beauty quite seriously. Especially valued is the imperfect in nature: gnarled, twisted, weathered forms are venerated as *go-shintai* (the abodes of deities) in Shinto, the indigenous religion of Japan. This appreciation of natural growth patterns is reflected in the rhythmic lines that have always distinguished Japanese art forms. In ikebana twisting and spiralling patterns of growth – the growth line – are all important. Leaves and blossoms are simply seen as embellishments of the stem and plant material is never massed to obscure the beauty of the stem itself.

Taking a closer look

Westerners do not have to adopt the entire Japanese cultural response to nature in order to enjoy and practise ikebana. All you need to do is to look more closely at the form and habits of growing plants. You need to be able to distinguish the differences between the forceful vertical energy of daffodils in spring, the ponderous nodding quality of a peony in summer and the wandering stark line of a bare branch in winter. The aim in ikebana is to accentuate the uniqueness of each material. Working with the essence of pattern in nature enables an arrangement to suggest so much with so little.

Ikebana is a seasonal art form: in general, plant materials from different times of year are rarely mixed. Ikebana also finds beauty in the transience of all things. Plant materials in all stages of their life are used. The bud, seed pod, battered leaf and lichen on a branch all reflect the changing seasons and the cycle of life and death. Much of the floral symbolism in ikebana derives from the principle that while plants change with the seasons, their innate quality remains constant.

Understanding a little more of the Japanese perception of beauty and nature makes it easier to understand one of ikebana's most distinctive characteristics – the use of space. In an ikebana design, space is just as important as the flowers and branches themselves. An ikebana practitioner seeks to create space rather than fill it. Space is an expressive part of the whole composition. It embraces the line and form of the individual plant materials, creating a dynamic tension. The observer's imagination is encouraged to complete what is incomplete, to make perfect what is not.

Viewer participation is important in ikebana. Whereas a western arrangement says 'look at me' or 'admire me', an ikebana design says 'engage with me' or 'consider me'. The use of fewer materials, asymmetrically placed and emphasizing the rhythm of line, draws the observer inwards. The arrangements resemble sculptures, gaining an extra presence beyond the merely decorative. The individual qualities of the flowers and plant materials express a range of emotions and seasons – suggestions of time past, present and future. Rather than simply bringing something of nature indoors, ikebana aims much higher: its intention is to suggest the whole of nature.

The art of placement

Ikebana is an art of placement. Plant materials are carefully placed according to firm rules of angle and measurement. These rules were developed by the Japanese flower masters, who were guided both by their study of nature and principles already employed in the visual arts – simplicity, expressiveness of line, asymmetry and the power of suggestion through understatement, encouraging observers to discover hidden beauty themselves. Contrary to what you might think, following the rules in ikebana does not produce identical work: instead it provides a springboard for creativity. The discipline of arranging materials with precision is very satisfying and the rules quickly become second nature.

Great importance is given to the activity itself and the state of mind of the ikebana practitioner.

One of Hokusai's 36 views of Fujiyama from the early nineteenth century showing Lake Sowa

Being relaxed yet focused is more important than enthusiasm, just as it is to work selflessly and with humility. Branches seem to snap and flowers wilt more quickly in the hands of someone who works with the force of their personality, or fusses too much. Ikebana is a great way to deal with stress and regular practice increases our ability to handle the events in our lives more resourcefully.

Japanese culture lays as much emphasis on developing gentleness of spirit as on improving the mind. This way of working is known as *hana-no-kokoro* or flower heart, and is seen as an achievement in its own right. It describes the heart-to-heart communication between flower and ikebana artist, between master and pupil and, ultimately the universal heart – our relationships with fellow human beings and all living things. Ikebana is a celebration of the connection between people and nature.

Today masters of ikebana are highly respected. The art form is taught by disciplined imitation of the work of the master. The calm, effortless movements with which a master builds an arrangement are inspiring to watch. Similarly, there are no words, no reasons given, when the master removes all the flowers in one swoop from the vase of a pupil. When the work is not right, the idea is to encourage the student to look more closely and use their own experience to discover why.

Everyone can enjoy the practice of ikebana, whatever their level of skill. It is an art form in which your own feelings and impressions of the flowers' beauty influence the arrangements you create. There is a distinct thrill that goes with a sense of mastery of the form – being able to conceive and construct something beautiful. Ikebana is an instant art form that offers immediate feedback.

History of ikebana

With the introduction of Buddhism to Japan via Korea and China in the sixth century, so too came the custom of *kuge* or offerings of flowers at the altar. A Buddhist priest named Ono-No-Imoko was dissatisfied with the careless way in which priests made flower offerings at the altar of the Buddha. He experimented with arrangements that symbolized the whole universe – a far more suitable offering. In his designs, flowers and branches reached upwards (never downwards) and were arranged in a group of three to represent the harmonious relationship between heaven, man and earth.

From the altar to the home

Priests continued to make flower arrangements for hundreds of years, but there are no records of any form of designs that followed a particular system until the late fifteenth century. At this time, simultaneously with the Renaissance in Italy, Japan experienced an explosion of artistic development, creating traditional Japanese architecture as we know it today, *haiku* poetry, *Noh* theatre and gardening.

Grand arrangements

The simple floral offerings for the altar evolved into a style called *rikka* or standing flowers. The earliest designs symbolized the mythical Mount Meru of Buddhism, the central mountain around which all creation sprang. These tall, formal arrangements became even grander as they made their way into the imperial courts of the Shogun, the ruling warlords. In the hands of noblemen, *doboshus* (priests) and *samurai* warriors, flower arranging became an erudite pastime. Designs representing landscapes were categorized according to moods: *shin* or formal, *gyo* or semi formal and *so*, informal. Up to nine different plant materials were used, with each branch having its own name, and a position in relation to the others. All the branches sprang from one

The eighth-century Daibutsu or Great Buddha at the Todai-ji Temple with an early formal flower arrangement.

Seventeenth-century rikka arrangement by Fushun-Ken Senkei, one of the last great rikka masters.

point, soaring gracefully like a tree, rooted in their heavy bronze containers. The arrangements were complicated and required a great deal of skill to construct; some were 15 feet high.

In contrast to the elaborate court arrangements, a more informal style was developing in conjunction with the tea ceremony. This was a ritual stressing simplicity and equality of all men. It was performed in a small, asymmetrical room, filled with natural materials and soft filtered light. The flowers and container needed to be unobtrusive, and as simple and as natural as possible. Often just one flower was used or an interesting branch; the state of mind of the artist was equally as important as the flowers themselves. The new-style tea ceremony

Late sixteenth-century arrangements by tea and flower masters

flowers were called either *chabana* (tea arrangement) or *nageire*, literally 'tossed into a pot' (see page 42).

Nageire became popular as less emphasis was placed on rules and more on the natural form of the flowers. Japanese sages were fond of saying that a peaceful generation may idly seek beauty in artificiality, but those born in an age of turmoil and war find satisfaction only in recreating the unstudied informality of nature herself.

The spread of ikebana

Throughout its history, ikebana has fluctuated between formal and informal styles. The seventeenth century saw the return to rikka as the most popular style of ikebana. Under the control of the Kyoto nobles, the rules of rikka meant that the art form could be regimented and controlled, which was much more difficult to do with the freer style of nageire.

In the eighteenth century, with the rise of the prosperous merchant classes, a form of nageire became popular. The wealthy merchants wanted a style of ikebana that was easier to learn than rikka to show off their best containers and decorate the *tokonoma* or living room alcove. Rather like the mantelpiece in the West, the *tokonoma* represents the heart of the home. While the Western hearth mainly signifies comfort, the tokonoma is viewed with additional respect because of its original use as the family altar. Today more decorative than useful or spiritual, it has evolved into a place to display objects of beauty. It occupies most of one side of the main room of the house, at right angles to the garden. The alcove is rectangular with two tall uprights and a cross-beam forming its frame.

The new style, called *seika* or *shoka*, meaning 'placid living flowers', consisted of a basic asymmetric triangular shape with its three main branches symbolizing heaven, man and earth (see page 18). It had some of the formality of rikka, but using only very few materials shows the influence of nageire. It was easy to do and was instrumental in introducing ikebana to all classes of society. For the first time women were encouraged to practise ikebana.

The influence of the West

Japan was forced to open up to trade for the first time when America sent ships to its ports in 1867. Suddenly Japan was flooded with new information. Foreign ideas were regarded as civilized and enlightened and were eagerly absorbed. Western-style interiors became fashionable and flowers such as dahlias, daisies and tulips were seen for the first time.

The first ikebana master to respond to these new influences was Unshin Ohara, who founded the Ohara School in 1895. Traditional ikebana arrangements for the tokonoma were designed to be seen from the front and when seated on

Woodblock by Suzuki Harunobu showing courtesans with a seika-style arrangment of narcissi displayed in the tokonoma

the floor, and he noted their uneasy transition to the new Western tables where people sat on chairs to look at them. Ohara combined his success as a sculptor with his classical training in ikebana to create a whole new style of ikebana as important as rikka and nageire. It was called *moribana* or 'piled-up flowers'.

In some ways, Ohara was rather like a Japanese impressionist and he shocked the ikebana establishment. He was inspired by the colour and form of the new flowers and designed shallow tray-like containers to show them at their best and most natural looking. Moribana's use of colour, ease of construction, expressive freedom and suitability for more locations within the home meant that it became very popular. Eventually it was accepted by the other main schools and taught together with nageire and rikka.

Ikebana is an enormously popular art practised by millions of people and is even part of the arts curriculum for Japanese school children. It is taught by more than three thousand different ikebana schools: the top three being Ikenobo, Ohara and Sogetsu. Ikenobo is the oldest of the three and most classical; Sogetsu is the most modern and emphasizes self-expression; Ohara draws on tradition in sourcing its modernity. That ikebana has survived and adapted over the centuries in Japan confirms its important role in today's society.

An early moribana arrangement with bulrushes and two species of water lily.

Ikebana today

Technological advances and sweeping urbanization have dulled our connection to the natural world. We must be increasingly goal driven to survive, yet this provokes concerns about health, well being and the quality of life. More than ever, the home is seen as a haven that protects and nurtures us. The popularity of feng shui, the ancient art of harmonizing man and environment, is evidence of our readiness to explore alternative attitudes to life.

The surge of interest in gardening and the desire to blur the boundaries between outdoors and indoors is another indication that we want to live in closer connection to nature. And one of the greatest hidden pleasures of ikebana is reserved for gardeners. Once you start to practise, you'll discover new plant patterns everywhere in your garden and notice things that had previously seemed insignificant. Ikebana is a perfect way to increase your appreciation of flowers. Through its practice you can develop your own flower heart, a much needed counterbalance to fast paced, stressful modern life.

Ikebana gives everyone the chance to be creative without being elitist or intimidating. Anyone who has ever thought that they were not artistic will be delighted at how quickly they begin to feel creative when they start studying ikebana. You don't even need a particular talent with flowers: success comes from practice.

Ikebana as sculpture

Ikebana is a sculptural art form highly suited to contemporary interiors. They share similar qualities: an emphasis on space, simplicity and clarity of line and form. In simple surroundings, ikebana's three-dimensional properties can have maximum impact, capturing the imagination and contributing to the atmosphere in the same way as a piece of sculpture.

Ikebana fits in with our increasing awareness of good design in the home because of its ability to enhance the mood and underlying structure of a space. It is so much more than decorating with flowers or adding the finishing touch to a room. Through its architectural structure and precise proportions, an ikebana arrangement enters into a dialogue with its surroundings, reinforcing the spatial and structural qualities of a living area.

Ikebana and interior design

At an aesthetic level, ikebana is fantastic training for the eye. It teaches you to see in a new way and to appreciate simplicity – skills that are valuable in all areas of design. Its aim to make life clearer urges the practitioner to use fewer materials to show the beauty of a line or shape more clearly. This in turn creates greater confidence in applying a similar approach to interiors. Once you've studied ikebana, it becomes easier to look at a room and decide what to add or take away.

Anyone interested in interior design will benefit enormously from taking a look at ikebana. The endless design variations that can be made from a small quantity of materials is in itself a source of inspiration when working with contemporary interiors. It opens up many new ways of expressing mood and conveying the beauty of nature within our homes – it's a source of fresh ideas.

Ikebana is supremely suited to the mood and tempo of life today. It is practical, beautiful and it doesn't take up a lot of time. As it uses far fewer materials than Western flower arrangements tend to, it doesn't cost much – next to nothing if you are lucky enough to have a garden. Ikebana produces the longest lasting results possible with cut materials, the result of centuries of experimentation by Japanese flower masters in the efficient handling and conditioning of flowers and woody branches.

A source of joy and satisfaction, ikebana is pleasure, pure and simple.

The techniques

The art of ikebana is governed by rules and these need to be mastered before you can produce pleasing arrangements. If this all sounds rather formal, bear in mind a quote from Sofu Teshigahara, the first headmaster of the Sogetsu School of ikebana, which opened in 1926. He encouraged his pupils with the words 'from formality comes freedom'.

What he was saying was that you have to learn the basic techniques in order to understand balance, shape and, most importantly, the concept of space. Ikebana rules help you focus your mind and concentrate on expressing ideas in an artistic form. Once learnt, they will stay with you for ever and then you will be free to create your own work.

The rules that you will learn here are fairly general but are loosely based on those taught by the Ohara School of ikebana.

The main lines in ikebana

The most important branches and flowers in an ikebana arrangement are known as the main lines or sometimes as the principal stems. They are the first plant materials to go into the arrangement and produce the underlying structure of the design.

All ikebana schools have different names for the main lines. This book uses the terms subject line, object and secondary line, which are the names used by the Ohara School. Sogetsu ikebana masters, for example, refer to the same lines as heaven, earth and man, respectively. On the following pages, every step-by-step guide to an arrangement will specify the lengths of the main lines.

Subject line

The first branch to be placed in the arrangement is the subject line or *shu*, meaning master. This is always the longest branch in a fixed arrangement. Its length is determined by the size of the container. The other pieces of plant material take their length from the subject line.

Object

The object or *kyaku*, which means guest, is often the first thing you notice when you look at an arrangement. It binds the whole arrangement together and forms a focus, while enhancing the beauty of the subject line. The object is nearly always a flower except in all-foliage arrangements, when it could be a cluster of new pieris leaves or a whole hosta plant, for example. The object can be supported by another piece of the same plant.

Secondary line

The secondary line or *fuku*, which translates as auxiliary, supports the subject line visually. In some arrangements, the subject and secondary are meant to look as if they are growing from the same point. As a rule of thumb, the secondary line is always shorter than the subject. Its exact length varies according to each arrangement.

Fillers

Once the main lines are in position, the fillers can be added. These are used to make an arrangement even more beautiful. Moribana arrangements (see page 33) specify the length, position and the number of fillers; in other designs, they can be added freely. In general, the longest filler should never be more than two-thirds the length of the subject line, while the shortest can be very short indeed. The main point to remember is that the filler should never be allowed to take over the whole

Measuring the subject line for a moribana arrangement

The standard length of the subject line in a moribana arrangement is equal to the depth plus the width of the container at its widest point.

1. The length of the branch overhanging the right hand side of the container is equivalent to the depth. In this example, the branch was held upside down against the container to measure it. To add on the width, roll the branch so that it lies across the container,

2. Cut off the excess on the left hand side of the branch, leaving a centimetre or two to go on the kenzan, and cutting the branch at a 45° angle (see page 20).

3. Put a kenzan or pin-holder (see page 20) in the container as shown. This branch was inserted at the back – the position for an upright moribana design.

Creating an upright moribana

1. The subject line – a ginger lily (*Heliconia*) – is the first to be added.

2. The subject and secondary – a second stem of ginger – in position.

3. Adding the object – an amaryllis (*Hippeastrum*).

4. Using fillers – stems of red bromeliad and an extra ginger lily plus leaf – to complete the upright moribana.

1

2

3

4

arrangement or overwhelm the object. Fillers should support the main lines and finish the arrangement.

Cutting stems to length

The length of the subject line is always determined by the container, either its width or height. For arrangements in shallow containers, take your flower or branch and lay it across the container at its widest point to judge where to cut it (see opposite). For flowers such as roses, daisies, tulips, lilies, chrysanthemums – in fact, any single-stemmed flower – take your measurements from the point where the petals join the stem. The given length excludes the size of the flower head.

Gladioli, delphiniums and any flowers that have a series of blooms arranged along one stem, can be measured in their entirety. Branches - bare or with leaves - also have their whole length taken into account.

There's no need to use a ruler, ikebana isn't about calculating lengths down to the nearest millimetre. Similarly, you can judge by eye the angles of the plant material given in the instructions. Everyone knows what a right angle is: 45° is half that distance, 30° a bit less.

Getting ready to make an arrangement

Now that the main lines of an arrangement have been explained, it's time to look at some designs. This section begins by looking at the simplest arrangements, gradually progressing to more complicated designs. The first arrangements use only two of the main lines described – the subject and the object. These are known as simple hana designs and also use just two types of plant material (see page 22). The next series of designs are known as moribana: they have three main lines and may use up to three types of plant material. Simple hana designs and moribana are both done in shallow dishes. The third style of arrangements, nageire, are characterised by being made in tall pots.

Before you start work, here are some simple tips and methods to help make your arrangements a success.

First things first

A good point to remember before starting an arrangement is that the space around the flower is equally important as the flower itself. You must leave some room for the 'breeze' to pass through and stir the branches. Some ikebana artists like to remind you to leave room for 'the birds and the butterflies', but the thought of a gentle wind is more calming and peaceful. Remember this and you'll be well on your way to a beautiful arrangement.

Before you begin, clear your mind completely and concentrate on the flowers, the plant material and nature itself. The process of creating an arrangement starts when you hold the branch in your hands and decide where to place it, following as closely as you can the way it grows in nature.

Ikebana means 'living flowers'. Yet when we cut branches and flowers we 'kill' them. By putting them in a beautiful arrangement and adding water, we give them back their life for a transitory period of time. Creating an arrangement should be a tranquil and thoughtful experience that you can immerse yourself in completely, forgetting everything else. In this way you give part of yourself to the design and add a very personal element to it.

Preparing your chosen plant material

Once you've chosen the material for your arrangement, you'll get the best results by re-cutting both flower stems and branches underwater. This is a process known as *mizugiri* or 'cutting stems underwater' to prevent air locks and allow free passage of water. Many plants and flowers need additional preparation or conditioning, but all materials will benefit from mizugiri. When you cut the stems, place the material immediately in a bucket of water and cut them again underwater. (See page 154 for more detailed instructions, plus conditioning techniques.)

Plant material often needs trimming before use to reveal or emphasize the line of a branch or stem. Small twigs near the base are usually removed and twigs that cross over. Stems with flowers in full bloom benefit from removing some leaves to highlight the flowers.

Cutting materials ready to use

The plants in ikebana are held in position on a *kenzan* or pin-holder, literally 'sword mountain'. There are different techniques for cutting material before placing it on the kenzan. Ikebana shears are called *hasami* and are very sharp with no spring: they will cut anything from a three-quarter inch branch to a daisy. If you can't get hold of a pair, use secateurs or scissors instead.

Cutting branches

Woody and hard branches must be cut at an angle and placed on the kenzan as shown in diagram 1. Branches up to 7mm (1/4 in) thick should be cut at 45°, in one movement. Thicker branches may take several cuts to slice through. The point of the cut branch goes onto the kenzan and is pushed firmly into position, initially upright. The angle of the branch is varied by increasing the pressure on the branch, as shown in diagram 2. Push the branch into position so that the cut side starts to face upwards. That way the kenzan will grab on to the solid uncut edge of the stem. If you don't follow this technique, the branch will fall over.

If the branch is very thick and heavy, make a cut

vertically up the centre of the stem as shown in diagram 3. This allows the kenzan to grab the branch in two places for extra support.

Cutting flowers and plants with soft stems

These are cut straight across in one swift, clean movement of the scissors and placed on the kenzan as shown in diagram 4. If soft material is not cut straight across, it will topple over.

Choosing a container

The container will depend on the arrangement you are doing. Suggestions for plant material plus appropriate dishes, pots or vases are given for each of the arrangements that follow. It is important to think about the container's colour, shape and even the meaning it holds for you. A favourite pot or vase can often produce your best work.

Fill the container with water only once you have finished adding the plant material. There are two exceptions: when making a nageire design in a tall pot, you must fill it first to give it stability; if it's a hot day, it's also a good idea to put some water in the bottom of a container while you are working.

Practising an arrangement

Reading instructions and starting your first arrangement can be daunting and it's easy to feel confused. Ikebana is a three-dimensional art and can be hard to visualize. Cut some twigs from the garden and use a lump of modelling clay or play dough for a pin-holder. Push the twigs into the positions of the main lines and practise angling them as specified in the arrangement. You'll soon get a feel for it. When you come to do your first arrangement for real, again practise first with spare branches or plant material.

When you've finished

Step back and look at your design. Can you see the lines of the arrangement clearly? If not, carefully trim it leaf by leaf and twig by twig until you feel happy with it.

diagram 1

diagram 2

diagram 3

diagram 4

Simple hana designs

Simple hana designs are based on just two main lines – the subject line and object. They also use just two plant materials. The word hana translates as flower, and these really are the simplest of all ikebana arrangements, but they are also extremely elegant. In a typical simple hana design, the stems all emerge from the same point in the arrangement.

Simple hana basic rising style

This style of ikebana uses plant material that reaches upwards. The main line is chosen from plant material that grows naturally skywards. It is a very simple arrangement but it has grace and elegance.

Choosing a container

The arrangement is set in the centre of a wide-mouthed *suiban* or shallow container. It doesn't have to be a special Japanese one, a plain pasta dish or a fruit or soup bowl will do. Here a small fruit bowl with a rich dark blue glaze was used. Choosing a container that reminds you of a special occasion or holiday, for example, will often give you extra inspiration. For this arrangement, you need to use a round kenzan to match the shape of the bowl.

Choosing plant materials

Look for a fairly long, reasonably straight branch or, as in this arrangement, a tall upright flower such as a gladiolus for the subject line. Delphiniums would be an alternative or you could even use the tall, straight leaves of crocosmia or iris. Then choose a flower to be the object or focus of the arrangement. The object forms the second main line of the design: in this case, it is a dark pink oriental lily.

This arrangement is based on just two plant materials. If you want to use fillers, these must be the same plants as the subject and the object.

Technique

Place the kenzan in the centre of the bowl. The first plant material to go into the container is the subject line. Cut the gladiolus to length by measuring it against the bowl. It should be twice the diameter of the bowl plus the depth. This length is a rule of thumb and may vary slightly with the size and shape of the container. Push the subject stem into the centre of the kenzan in an upright position, but it may lean 20° in any direction (see diagram 1). How you tilt the subject depends on the shape of the branch or flower. Look carefully at it and note any bends and twists. Once you start to experiment, you'll find a position where it looks best within the angle of 20°.

The next line to add is the object, in this case the lily. Its stem should measure one third of the length of the subject line. It goes on the kenzan at an angle of 45° to the vertical, as shown in diagram 1. Once in position, the object may also point a maximum of 20° to the left or right (see diagram 2).

Once the two main lines are in place, fillers can be added. In this example, a second gladiolus forms a supporting filler for the subject and an extra lily plus bud is used to emphasize the object. In these basic arrangements, you can place the fillers freely, where you want them, and you can decide their length. Just remember not to introduce any new plant types – stick to lilies and gladioli.

LENGTHS OF THE MAIN LINES

Subject: twice the diameter of the container plus the depth

Object: one-third length of subject

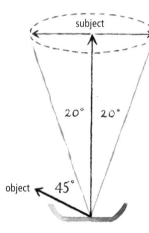

Diagram 1 side view

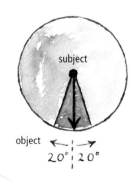

Diagram 2 bird's eye view

subject

object

LENGTHS OF THE MAIN LINES
Subject: one and a half times the width of the container
Object: one third the length of the subject

Simple hana variation of basic rising style

This arrangement also uses upward growing plant material, and again only two plant materials and two main lines. The difference comes from the change of position of the design, by moving the kenzan to the left or right of the suiban.

Choosing a container

You need a shallow container with a flat bottom so that the kenzan can be moved to the left or right. This example uses a smart black bowl bought in a high street store: it is oblong in shape with rounded corners and shines like polished coal. The kenzan is also an oblong design that fits into the corner of the suiban.

Choosing plant materials

Look for plant material that grows naturally upwards for the subject, just as you did for the simple hana basic rising style. The subject line needs to be a little shorter this time to balance the shift of the design to the side of the container.

The object is still the focus of the arrangement but this time it is placed at the side. As in the basic rising style, the fillers must be in the same two materials as the subject line and object.

In this example, a stem of bells of Ireland (*Molucella laevis*) with its curious green flowers forms the subject line. A cheerful garden marigold (*Calendula officinalis*) is the object. Both of these species are common garden

flowers that are easy to grow. They are also popular cut flowers and are readily available from florists.

Technique

Position the kenzan to the left of the container. This time cut the subject line so that it is approximately one and a half times as long as the width of the container. Place the subject in the far back left corner of the kenzan, tilting it up to 20° in any direction. Just as before, in the basic rising style, you will find that the subject – in this case, the bells of Ireland – will look right to you in one particular position (see diagram 1).

The object needs to be a third of the length of the subject line. Position the object – the marigold – in front of the subject line. Insert it at the base of the subject and at an angle of 45° to the vertical (see diagram 1). The position of the object can vary by up to 20° to the right or left (see diagram 2).

Now that the two main lines are in place, you can add the marigold fillers and a supporting stem of bells of Ireland to complete the arrangement.

As before, you can use the fillers freely. Just remember that the object should have the biggest and best bloom, so when you add the marigold fillers, make sure they don't detract from the marigold object. Similarly, the second stem of bells of Ireland should be slightly shorter than the one that forms the subject line, to avoid dominating the arrangement.

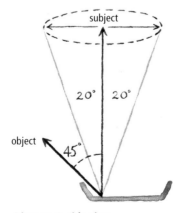

Diagram 1 side view

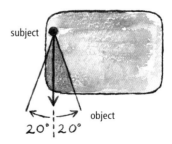

Diagram 2 bird's eye view

Simple hana basic slanting style

This arrangement still uses two main lines and two types of plant material. It is designed to make the most of graceful slanting materials and the subject must be a plant that grows that way naturally.

Choosing a container

Traditionally, the simple hana basic slanting style is done in a suiban or shallow container, although it looks equally good in deeper bowls. The stems all radiate from the centre of the container and, just as in the basic rising style, a shallow fruit or soup bowl is ideal. The arrangement here is a good choice for small containers. It stands in a small black dish that is approximately 15cm (6in) in diameter, but it could even be done in a tea-cup. Choose a round kenzan to go with the container.

Choosing plant materials

Azaleas, flowering quince (*Chaenomeles japonica*) and acers grow naturally at wonderful angles and, as always in basic ikebana, the branches are used in the way in which they grow. Here an acer branch forms the subject line. This branch has lichen growing on it, which contributes to the texture of the design.

The object is a yellow calla lily (*Zantedeschia aethiopica*), tinged with coral red inside. The colour of the lily tones with the tints of the acer leaves, but the lily is still the focus of the arrangement.

Technique

Place the kenzan in the centre of the container. Cut the subject line – the acer – so that it measures about twice the width of the dish or a little less. Its position is best explained by looking at diagram 1. The container is divided into sectors and the subject line can go anywhere in the back 270° sector. (The total number of degrees in a circle is, of course, 360.) The acer branch comes out from the centre of the kenzan and over the side of the container. The angle it is placed at can range from 60° to a little less than 90° to the vertical, as shown in diagram 2.

Cut the object – the calla lily – so that it is a third of the length of the subject line. Place it in the centre of the remaining 90° sector, as indicated in diagram 1. You can then vary its position by moving it a maximum of 20° to the left or right. The angle of slant of the object is 45° to the vertical.

Use some more acer leaves and another calla lily as fillers where you feel they are needed. The second calla lily used here is in bud and so does not overwhelm the object lily – an important consideration.

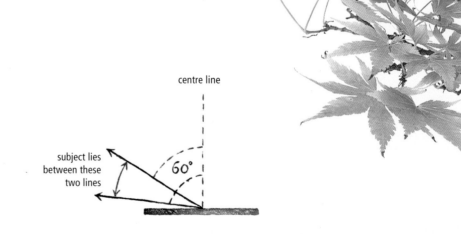

Diagram 1 bird's eye view

270°

subject

object

20° 20°

centre line

subject lies between these two lines

60°

Diagram 2 angle of slant for the subject

LENGTHS OF THE MAIN LINES

Subject: about twice the width of the container or a little shorter

Object: one third the length of the subject

LENGTHS OF THE MAIN LINES

Subject: one and a half times the width of the container

Object: one third the length of the subject

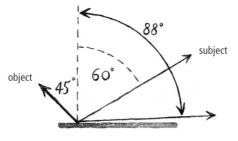

Diagram 1 side view

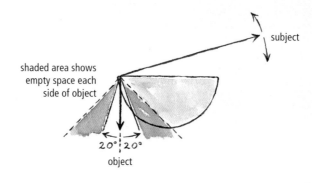

Diagram 2 bird's eye view with kenzan on the left of the semi-circular container

Simple hana variation of basic slanting style

This is the last of the two-line two-material arrangements in this section of the book. You need a flat-bottomed container so that you can move the kenzan to the right or left. This is a style that lends itself to very modern work.

Choosing a container

This arrangement uses a traditional Japanese container called a *shohinka*. It is shallow and semi-circular, and its raised foot gives the feeling of more space under the arrangement. If you use this type of dish, you'll need a triangular kenzan that will fit into either end of the half-circle. The triangular kenzan is called a *ginkgo* after the leaves of the ginkgo tree, which are similar in shape. Using a matt black container highlights the modern design.

The arrangement works equally well in an ordinary shallow, flat-bottomed bowl, such as a soup or fruit bowl, which will still allow you to move the kenzan from left to right as necessary.

Choosing plant material

The bold leaves of the fatsia (*Fatsia japonica*) grow naturally at an angle and are ideal for a variation of the basic slanting style. You need strong flowers to complement them – oriental lilies are a good match.

Technique

Place the kenzan on the left of the container. Cut the subject line – the fatsia leaf – so that it is one and a half times the width of the container. Place it on the back of the kenzan. As in the basic slanting style, the subject can go anywhere in the back 270° sector, behind the dotted lines (see diagram 2). The subject can swing out at an angle of anything from 60 to 88° to the vertical (see diagram 1). In this example, the fatsia leaf slants about 75° to the vertical.

Cut the object – the lily – so that it is one third of the length of the subject line. Insert it at the base of the subject, at an angle of 45° to the vertical. As in the basic slanting style, it can also move up to 20° left or right.

Now add the fillers – another fatsia leaf and extra lilies. As before, you can add them freely, as long as you don't overwhelm the object flower.

object

subject

How to use simple hana designs

Start using your new skills to make simple arrangements for your home and you will soon gain in confidence. Here is an ideal design for a bathroom. While a bathroom can be a place to relax, it also needs to be practical. Given the room's importance and typical modern-day restrictions on space, arrangements for a bathroom are best kept small and simple.

The basic rising style was chosen for its absolute simplicity. The vertical iris leaves are the subject line and a delicate pink hydrangea (*Hydrangea macrophylla*) forms the object. Extra iris leaves and a second hydrangea flower are used as fillers.

Both materials were picked from the garden, providing an instant connection with the outside and the feel-good factor of creating something beautiful from readily available, everyday materials.

The iris leaves and hydrangea work so effectively together through contrast – the vigorous vertical line of the sharp iris leaves versus the soft hydrangea flowers. Little arrangements like this really shine and gain extra presence if you display them on their own small table. The tinted glass table top reflects a diffuse pink light onto the underside of the shallow white household bowl, enhancing the delicacy and freshness of the pink hydrangea flowers. It is placed so that it can be seen on entering the room, as well as being appreciated from the bath tub.

Introduction to moribana

Moribana literally means 'piled-up flowers'. This expressive style of using plant materials and flowers was introduced at the beginning of the twentieth century by Unshin Ohara, the first headmaster of the Ohara School (see page 12).

The designs are made in shallow containers and the style of arrangement is largely determined by the plant materials available. The moribana arrangements described here are the basis for many more complicated and exciting designs that will be illustrated later in the book. All of these will be easier to understand if you master the rules and techniques of moribana first.

Moribana designs are based on three main lines. The third important line, known as the secondary, is added to the subject line and object.

One of the main differences between moribana and simple hana designs is the position of the stems on the kenzan. In simple hana designs the stems are grouped together on the kenzan. In moribana, they are arranged in a scalene triangle. This is a triangle with unequal sides and the three main lines are inserted at each point of the triangle. As well as using three main lines, moribana designs use a maximum of three plant materials and they also have three positions for inserting the plant material that is used for fillers.

The various styles of moribana arrangements are produced by changing the position and angle of the subject and secondary lines on the kenzan. When the kenzan is positioned on the left of the suiban, so that the plant material is inserted on the left of the container, the arrangement is described as *hongatte*. In general, arrangements and instructions are usually given as hongatte unless otherwise stated.

The opposite to hongatte is *gyakugatte,* when the kenzan is on the right of the container and plant material is inserted from the right. The plant material itself – its angle of growth, its shape – is the deciding factor that determines whether you make a hongatte arrangement or a gyakugatte one.

The three basic styles of moribana explained on these pages are the upright style, the slanting style and the water-reflecting style.

LENGTHS OF THE MAIN LINES

Subject: the length of the container plus the depth (the moribana standard length)

Secondary: two thirds the length of the subject

Object: half the length of the subject

subject

tall filler

valley filler

secondary

object

short filler

Moribana upright style

This is perhaps the simplest moribana arrangement and it is the one students usually learn first. There are three fixed positions for the main lines and fillers, and a maximum of three plant materials can be used. The arrangement is designed to be viewed from the front.

Choosing a container

Use a wide-mouthed, flat-bottomed container that allows the kenzan to be moved from left to right, so you can choose whether to make a hongatte or gyakugatte arrangement.

The colour of the container is important. In this arrangement a matt black dish enhances the plant material used and highlights the colours. Its size gives balance to the whole composition, which is set at the back of the container, so that you look right across the dish and into the arrangement.

Choosing plant material

As the style suggests, plant material for the subject and secondary lines must grow naturally upright. This design is often done all in single-stemmed chrysanthemums and is the basis for special traditional work.

In this example, fantastic fox tail lilies (*Eremurus*) form the subject and secondary lines. Gladioli, ginger lilies (*Heliconia*) or upright branches such as Irish yew (*Taxus baccata* 'Fastigiata') would also look good. The object is a single-stemmed chrysanthemum bloom in a deep rust colour. It has to be a strong flower – fox tail lilies are very dominant. Supporting the chrysanthemum bloom with a second one makes the object even stronger.

The fillers are St John's wort berries (*Hypericum*) in an intense shade of orange. For natural harmony, the whole arrangement has been designed using autumn colours.

Technique

Place an oblong kenzan on the left of the suiban and work in the shaded area of the kenzan (see diagram 2). Cut a fox tail lily for the subject line. It should be the length of the container plus the depth. This is known as the standard length in moribana. Insert it at the back of the kenzan, upright but leaning slightly forward.

The secondary is another fox tail lily, two-thirds the length of the subject. Position it to the left of the subject at an angle of 45° from the vertical (see diagram 1). Let it point to the left about 30° as in diagram 2.

The object needs to be half as long as the subject line. Insert it in the front right hand corner of the kenzan to complete the scalene triangle. The object points 45° to the right and is inserted at an angle of 60° from the vertical (see diagrams 1 and 2). Tuck the second chrysanthemum in behind it.

The berried fillers can be inserted next. Although these have no set lengths, a general rule of thumb has been included to help you get the balance of the arrangement right. In the upright style, the tall filler is approximately half the length of the subject and is placed between the subject and the object. The valley filler is about a third of the length of the subject and goes between the subject and the secondary. Finally the short filler is about a third of the length of the secondary. Place it between the secondary and the object.

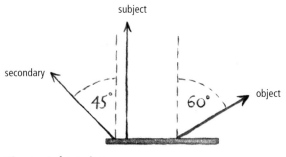

Diagram 1 front view

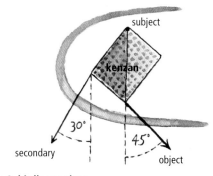

Diagram 2 bird's eye view

Moribana slanting style

This expressive form of moribana is used to emphasize the beauty of slanting or inclining material. Studying bare branches in winter gives an idea of their shape and structure. The branches used in ikebana usually dictate the style of an arrangement. The slanting moribana is a good example, as it uses naturally curving branches that sweep out from the side of the suiban. These are balanced by the piled-up flowers arranged closer to the centre.

Choosing a container
Some schools have special moribana containers to teach this arrangement. But once you've mastered the proportions and angles of insertion, you can use any flat-bottomed dish. A pasta dish is ideal, but use a plain one to avoid detracting from your design. Here an Ohara suiban called a *madoka* has been used, with an oblong kenzan that can be moved to the left or right.

Choosing plant material
Bare acer branches are used for the subject and secondary lines: in moribana arrangements these two lines are usually in the same plant material. Other options include slanting branches of camellia, flowering quince (*Chaenomeles japonica*) or apple blossom. The object is an eye-catching white chrysanthemum bloom and the fillers are extra pieces of acer with leaves, plus river-bank grasses. The object bloom can be supported by a second one, cut shorter and set in behind. When doing an arrangement limited to three types of plant material, the bare acer branches and the acer leaves count as one material, even though they are used separately and look quite different.

Technique
Place the kenzan on the left side of the suiban, just as you did for the upright moribana (see diagram 1). As before, work in the shaded area of the kenzan.

The first branch to go on the kenzan is the subject line, a bare acer branch one and a half times the length of the container. Place it at an angle of 70° from the vertical, then angle it out at 45° to the left, as in diagram 1.

The secondary line, also a bare acer branch, is half the length of the subject line. Insert it upright at the back of the kenzan, as in diagram 2.

Choose a large open chrysanthemum bloom for the object. The object is half the length of the subject line and tilts at about 45 or 50° degrees from the vertical (see diagram 2). As this is a hongatte arrangement, the kenzan is on the left and the object points to the right about 30° (see diagram 1). Before you add the fillers, you can add a second chrysanthemum flower, tucked in behind the first, to strengthen the arrangement.

Now add the fillers. In this arrangement, as in the moribana rising style, there are three positions for them: tall, short and valley fillers. Lengths of the fillers need only be approximate and can vary according to the plant material used. Tall fillers should be around two thirds the length of the subject, while the short and valley fillers are one third of the subject's length.

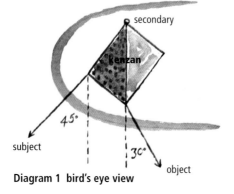

Diagram 1 bird's eye view

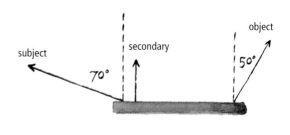

Diagram 2 front view

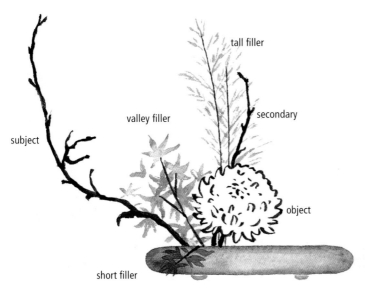

tall filler

valley filler

secondary

subject

object

short filler

LENGTHS OF THE MAIN LINES

Subject: one and a half times the length of the container

Secondary: half the length of the subject

Object: half the length of the subject

Moribana water-reflecting style

A graceful arrangement like this makes everyone stop and look. The subject branch sweeps low across the suiban to reflect in the water it holds. Using naturally low-growing material accentuates the design.

Choosing a container

To get the full effect of this arrangement, you need a fairly large container with a flat base. Space is needed for the overhanging branch and, as for other moribana designs, you must be able to move the kenzan to the right or to the left of the suiban. This suiban is dark blue and rectangular. Its shape exposes a large area of clear water for the reflection.

Choosing plant material

A branch of azalea sweeps across the water and forms the subject line for this arrangement. Another azalea branch forms the secondary line. Acer, camellia, low-growing pine and even mulberry branches would also be suitable. The object is a rich purple clematis, while the fillers are lime-green hosta leaves and extra clematis. The hosta leaves accentuate the clematis flowers, bringing them forward in the arrangement.

Technique

In this example of water-reflecting style, the kenzan is placed on the right-hand side of the container, making this a gyakugatte arrangement.

The subject line is one and a half times the length of the container. It sweeps low over the water at an angle of 70 to 80° to the vertical, crossing the container diagonally from the back right-hand corner to the front left (see diagrams 1 and 2). The secondary line is half as long as the subject line and is placed behind the subject, tilting slightly to the right (see diagram 1).

The clematis, which forms the object, should also be half as long as the subject line. It can be as low as 70 to 80° to the vertical (see diagram 1), with the flower facing forward. The flower also points out to the right at an angle of about 30°, to balance the heavy sweep to the left of the azalea branch (see diagram 2).

Add the fillers – the extra clematis flowers and the hosta leaves – between the main lines.

LENGTHS OF THE MAIN LINES
Subject: one and a half times the length of the container
Secondary: half the length of the subject
Object: half the length of the subject

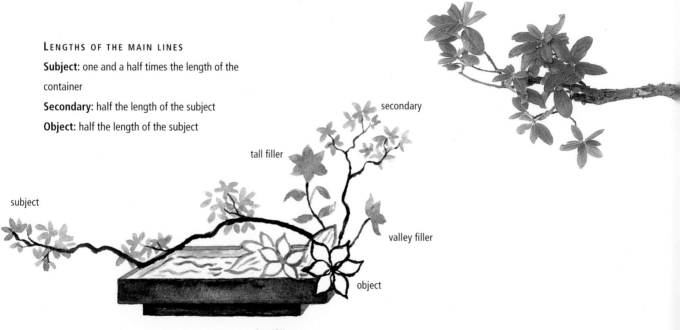

subject

tall filler

secondary

valley filler

object

short filler

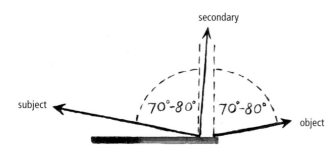

secondary

subject

object

70°-80° 70°-80°

Diagram1 front view

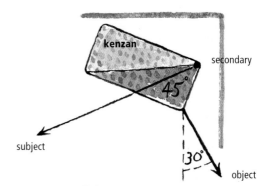

kenzan

secondary

subject

45°

30°

object

Diagram2 bird's eye view

How to use moribana designs

The starting point of this arrangement was the shape of the autumn materials to hand, specifically the curved sweep of the pyracantha branch, which suggested the water-reflecting moribana design. Hovering low over the water, the pyracantha is the subject line. It sweeps from left to right, making it a hongatte arrangement. Trimming off some of the leaves at the base reveals more of the line of the branch.

Looking to create space rather than fill it, the design is given balance by the secondary line – another pyracantha branch – reaching to the left at the back. The red tinge of the leaves influenced the choice of the other autumnal materials: a red dahlia for the object, supported by a second one cut shorter and inserted behind it; plus fillers of hypericum berries and dahlia buds.

The water-reflecting style is designed to be seen from the front, so placing it where you can't walk round it is no bad thing. When using branches that extend to the side, it is always advisable to allow plenty of space around the arrangement so its impact is unimpaired and its spatial qualities can be fully appreciated.

The container is a matt black suiban set on top of an old trunk against a wall. The overall effect is not too heavy, as a white mother-of-pearl mat reflects light onto the arrangement and throws the pyracantha into sharp relief.

Introduction to nageire

Nageire is an arrangement done in a tall pot or vase, which can be ceramic, pottery, glass or indeed any other kind of material. The style has its roots in chabana, flowers for the tea ceremony (see page 11). The literal meaning of the word nageire is 'tossed into the pot' and the arrangements have a very free feel to them – the rules are offered more as guidelines to help with balance of the arrangement. Nageire designs still have three main lines – subject line, secondary line and object – but need special fixings to keep the branches in place. The arrangements express the thoughts of the artist, and are designed to lift the spirits of both artist and observer.

Fixings for nageire arrangements

Instead of a kenzan, stays and supports are used to hold the branches in place. Some are used under the rim of the vase to hold a branch or stem, while others are longer pieces that act as a counterbalance to a branch. A cross piece is often inserted in the mouth of the pot, dividing it into quarters. Working within one of these smaller sections creates more space in an arrangement. It also allows you to make either hongatte designs on the left of the container, or gyakugatte designs on the right.

The design opposite uses berried hawthorn branches (*Crataegus monogyna*), acer leaves and *Leucadendron* 'Safari Sunset' foliage.

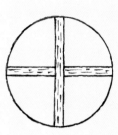

green wood cross
piece in place

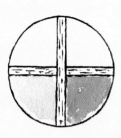

hongatte
arrangement
on left

gyakugatte
arrangement
on right

Diagram 1 cross piece method, bird's eye view of top of container.
Shaded areas show hongatte and gyakugatte positions

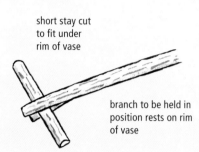

short stay cut
to fit under
rim of vase

branch to be held in
position rests on rim
of vase

Diagram 2 short stay method

Cross-piece fixings

These are the simplest fixings, inserted across the top of
the pot. You can make them yourself by cutting them
from flexible green wood, which will bend before it
cracks. Cut a branch fresh from a tree or bush, at least
13mm (1/2 in) in diameter. You can use the same
material that you will be making the arrangement from,
if you have plenty. If not, try hazel or ash branches. Trim
the branch so that it is slightly wider than the diameter
of the pot, then split it with your shears, so that you
end up with two pieces, each with one flat side and
one rounded. It is important to cut the ends of cross
pieces to fit the line of the inside of the container.

Slip the cross pieces under the rim of the vase, flat
side down and with the angled ends tight against the
side of the container. Pull them up into position, where
they should be firm and strong. The cross pieces don't
need attaching to each other but are placed at right
angles, one above the other (see diagram 1).

These can be used in all nageire designs and are
always used in the upright style.

Fixing slanting branches – short stay method

Slanting branches need to be fixed in place because
they don't reach to the bottom of the container. There
are two methods of fixing them. The first uses a short
stay inserted in the end of the branch. Start by cutting

the end of your branch to fit the line of the inside of
the container. Make the stay from a piece of another
branch about half the thickness of the branch you are
using in the arrangement. Or you can use a piece
trimmed from your original branch, slit in half vertically.
Cut the stay so that it is slightly wider than the
diameter of the vase.

Then make a slit in the branch you are using in the
arrangement and insert the stay so that it is horizontal
(see diagram 2). At this point, adjust the branch so that it
slants at the angle you need for the arrangement. If the
branch is strong it should hold the stay in place. If not,
use a short length of florist's wire to bind it in place.

Trim the stay to the right length and slip it under the
rim of the container, putting one end in first, then the
other and pulling it up tight under the rim. Now the
branch will be supported in three places: the branch
itself rests on the edge of the pot and the two ends of
the stay will hold it firmly under the rim.

Fixing slanting branches – long stay method

The second method of holding a branch in a tall pot
uses a long stay as a counterbalance. When you have
chosen your branch for the arrangement, cut the end
of the stem to fit the line of the inside of the vase. Then
cut a branch the same height as the vase to form the
long stay. Use fresh, green springy wood if possible.

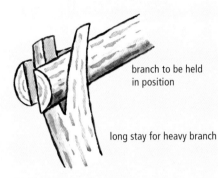

branch to be held
in position

long stay for heavy branch

Diagram 3 long-stay method

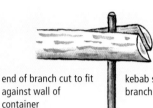

end of branch cut to fit
against wall of
container

kebab stick inserted into
branch

Diagram 4 kebab stick counterbalance

Slit the base of the branch for your design and insert the long stay vertically. Adjust the branch so that it slants at the angle needed for the arrangement. If necessary, use a short length of florist's wire to hold the stay firmly in position. Cut the bottom end of the stay so that it is flat and will sit solidly on the base of the pot.

Choose a thick branch as a long stay for heavy branches. For extra stability, you can secure both branch and stay by slitting both stems and interlocking them together (see diagram 3). Adjust the angle of the branch by pulling it down on to the stay. If necessary, you can then wire it to keep it in position.

For lighter, thinner material, a slender camellia branch, for example, you can use a wooden kebab stick as a counterbalance instead of a long stay. Split the branch as before and slot the kebab stick into the cut vertically and initially at right angles, until you adjust the branch to the angle specified. Wire the stick to the branch if necessary and then cut the point off the top of the kebab stick so that it will fit under the rim of the container without rolling (see diagram 4).

Depending on the size of the container, the kebab stick may reach the bottom of the pot. If it does, make a 'foot' at the bottom of the stick to stabilize it. Crack the bottom of the kebab stick without breaking it completely and fold over the end at right angles to form the foot. In larger containers, the kebab stick will slant across the

inside of the pot and touch the opposite side of the pot to the branch, so forming a counterbalance.

Holding flowers in place

Flower stems are generally too thin to take a stay to keep them in place, but there is a simple way to keep the flowers just where you want them. Cut the stem long then measure it against the container to get the length needed for the arrangement. Crack the stem at this point to leave at least 10-12.5cm (4-5in) to form a counterbalance that will hang down the back of the vase. If the counterbalance is too short, the flower could topple over.

To keep the flower in place, all you need to do is rest the counterbalance against the side of the vase. Then slide the stem up or down against the side of the vase to adjust the angle of the flower in the arrangement. Push it down to move the flower head up and vice versa. If you use this method, you must always make sure the crack in the stem is underwater.

Long-stemmed blooms that reach to the bottom of the vase can be stabilized in the same way by cracking the stem close to the end to form a short foot.

You can even insert a kebab stick vertically into the stem of a flower – a rose, for example – to make the stem longer, provided the join is kept under water. For stability, crack the kebab stick to form a short foot.

Nageire upright style

This arrangement uses material that grows straight up, to make a tall pot look even taller. This is a dynamic design with enormous impact on the observer.

Choosing a container

All ikebana schools have their own pots for nageire arrangements. This one is a design from the Ohara School called a *heika*. But you can, of course, use your own container. Choose a tall pot with an open mouth and a pronounced rim under which you can fix your chosen branches.

Choosing plant material

The lengths given for the main lines – subject, secondary and object – are all expressed as the length of the plant material that appears above the rim of the vase. Upright stems need to reach to the bottom of the vase for stability, so always remember to add another container-length of stem to the measurements for upright subject lines. In this arrangement, the length of the subject line above the rim of the vase must be one and a half times the height of the vase. So the actual length of the subject line will be two and a half times the vase's height.

An upright nageire arrangement can use up to three plant materials, but the subject and the secondary lines must be the same plant. Irish yew (*Taxus baccata* 'Fastigiata') with its combination of greens and yellows and rich texture forms the subject and secondary lines here. Gladioli and delphiniums would work well too – you don't have to use branches. The object is a large bronze chrysanthemum bloom with a curly texture. Two more chrysanthemum flowers slightly smaller than the object have been used as fillers, but you can introduce a third plant material if you prefer.

Technique

Start by putting two cross pieces in the top of the pot, to divide the mouth into quarters to work in. Then fill the pot with water. Never attempt a nageire arrangement without water in the container or the weight of the branches will topple the whole thing over.

This is a hongatte arrangement, so make the arrangement in the front left-hand quarter of the vase mouth. Insert the subject line first (see diagrams 1 and 2). It is one and a half times the height of the container, the nagiere standard length for upright and slanting subject lines. The subject leans slightly forward at about 15°. No extra fixing should be necessary because this branch should reach the bottom of the container.

Cut the branch of Irish yew that forms the secondary line so that it is two-thirds the length of the subject line. Insert it at approximately 60° to the vertical. Tuck it in just beside or behind the subject line so that it points about 30° to the left (see diagrams 1 and 2). Both lines should appear to be growing together.

The secondary line is almost certain to need a fixing: when choosing one, take into consideration the weight and the shape of the branch and the angle of insertion. In this case, a long stay was used to cope with the weight of the heavy yew branch.

Nageire arrangements are much less rigid than others and so, if the original left-hand quarter of the vase becomes crowded, you can shift the secondary line into the front of the back quarter to release some space.

Now add the fillers, all in the front left quarter. Again choose fixings for the fillers if they are needed. Here, one stem was long enough to reach the bottom of the pot but the other one rested on the cross pieces.

The object should be half the length of the subject. It comes forward at an angle of about 80° to the vertical: crack the stem to form a foot to hold it in place against the side of the vase or the cross piece. The object is strengthened visually by the long fillers behind.

When the arrangement is finished you should be able to move your hand across the whole of the right side of the arrangement: it should all be empty space.

Finally top up the container with water, at the same time making sure that all cut ends of branches and flowers are underwater.

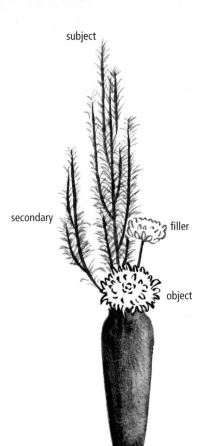

subject

secondary

filler

object

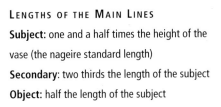

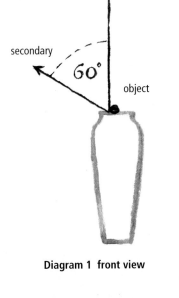

subject

secondary

60°

object

Diagram 1 front view

LENGTHS OF THE MAIN LINES

Subject: one and a half times the height of the vase (the nageire standard length)

Secondary: two thirds the length of the subject

Object: half the length of the subject

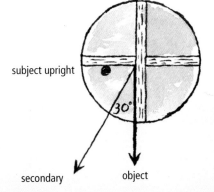

subject upright

30°

secondary

object

Diagram 2 bird's eye view, working on the left

The techniques 47

filler

secondary

subject

object

LENGTHS OF MAIN LINES

Subject: one and a half times the height of the vase (the nageire standard length)

Secondary: half the length of the subject

Object: half the length of the subject

vertical line

secondary

subject

70° 60°

object

Diagram 1 front view

Nageire slanting style

As in slanting moribana, this style of nageire is designed to show the beauty of naturally slanting plant material, which should appear to be still growing. You can't substitute vertical material and slant it at an angle – it would simply look as if it had fallen over.

In this arrangement there is a balance between the branches and the flowers. The subject line sweeps out over the side of the tall container with a lot of space below. The line of this branch also points forward, as though it is going over your shoulder, while the object comes towards you.

Choosing a container

Choose a tall pot and add one or two cross pieces to divide the mouth. You need to work in one quarter or one half of the space. How you decide which to do depends on the size of the mouth of the pot and the thickness of the branches being used. This arrangement was done in the left-hand half of the container as the plant material stems are quite thick. The container is an Ohara *heika* pot, which has a fairly wide mouth with a rim to hold the fixings in place.

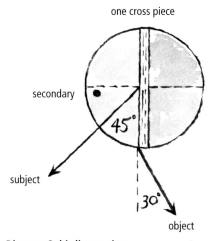

Diagram 2 bird's eye view

Choosing plant material

Acer, azalea and japonica branches all grow in a graceful slanting fashion. But you can often find slanting branches of less obvious choices of trees and shrubs by studying them carefully. Magnolias and camellias often yield such branches. Here azalea branches in autumn colours form the subject and secondary lines.

The object is a beautiful oriental white lily, which forms a sharp contrast to the highly coloured acer. You have a choice of fillers for this arrangement. They can either be in the same material as the subject line or the object or in a third material if you wish.

Technique

First insert a single cross piece and fill the pot with water. Cut the subject line to the nageire standard length (one and a half times the height of the container). The subject line is usually heavy and needs a long stay to act as a counterbalance. This a hongatte arrangement, so insert the subject in the front left-hand side, at an angle of 70° to the vertical and pointing 45° to the left (see diagrams 1 and 2).

The secondary is half the length of the subject line. Add it upright, behind the subject, tipping slightly backwards and to the left (see diagram 1).

Then add your chosen fillers – in this case, an extra lily bud, which appears tucked behind the object. The stem was long enough to reach the bottom of the pot, so no fixings were needed. Then add the object, which is half the length of the subject. Insert it pointing 30° to the right and at an angle of 60° from the vertical (see diagrams 1 and 2). This flower has a much shorter stem and it is held in place using the cracked stem method.

LENGTHS OF THE MAIN LINES
Subject: more than one and a half times the height of the vase
Secondary: half the nageire standard length of one and a half times the height of the container
Object: half the nageire standard length

secondary

filler

filler

object

secondary

object

45°

130°

Diagram 1 front view

subject

subject

high base

Nageire cascading style

In mountains or by the sea, plants often appear to be growing out of the rock face. The cascading nageire has its origin in these precariously clinging plants. They are often painted on Japanese screens and are thought to have a particular beauty. To produce this effect, the plant material cascades gracefully over the side of the container, usually standing on a tall base.

Choosing a container

An Ohara heika pot in pale turquoise is in perfect harmony with the blue pine. The container is standing on a base to add even more height and allow the plant material to cascade even further.

Choosing plant material

There are plenty of examples of cascading material, such as weeping willow (*Salix purpurea* 'Pendula') and cascading silver pear (*Pyrus salicifolia*). Many pine trees grow in this way and this example uses a beautiful blue pine for the subject and secondary lines. They are placed so close together that the secondary appears to grow out of the subject line.

The object and fillers are Colombian roses with large, heavy heads. Their shade of pink has a lot of blue in it and harmonizes with the blue pine.

The materials used in this arrangement have a special meaning: roses and pine used together symbolize everlasting peace.

Technique

Insert the cross pieces. Again, you may use one or two, depending on the thickness of the branches you are using. This arrangement uses just one. Then fill the pot with water.

The branch that forms the subject in this arrangement is usually fairly heavy and so you need to use a strong stay as a counterbalance. In this design, the subject line is more than one and a half times the height of the pot (the standard nageire length). You can decide on the final length, guided by the visual balance of the arrangement, as well as the physical balance.

Insert the subject line on the left to make a hongatte arrangement. It cascades down over the container at an angle of 130° to the vertical and points 45° to the left (see diagrams 1 and 2).

The secondary line is half the nageire standard length (see above) for slanting and upright subjects. This line goes into the arrangement behind the subject in an upright position but tilting slightly backwards. Use a fixing to hold it in place. This is a lighter branch and a kebab-stick counterbalance should be strong enough to hold it in position.

Fillers can be either pine, roses or a third material. Here they are all tall roses inserted behind the object. The tallest stem was long enough to reach the bottom of the pot; the other one was held against the back of the pot using the cracked stem technique.

The object is also half the nageire standard length and is inserted at an angle of 45° to the vertical and points right 30° (see diagrams 1 and 2). The cracked stem technique was used to get the angle right. Finally, top up the container with water.

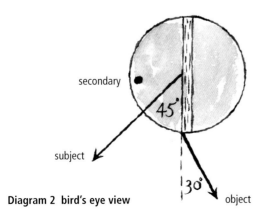

Diagram 2 bird's eye view

How to use nageire designs

Exotic branches of pomegranate fruit and blossom were the starting point for this arrangement. The dramatic downward drop of the pomegranates immediately pointed to a nageire cascading style, while the fruit itself suggested creating an arrangement for the kitchen – rather than the living room, for example. The strong shades of orangey-red prompted the choice of an equally intense complementary dark green container.

A cascading nageire design should always be placed in a fairly high position so that the main branch may cascade down to its full length, especially, of course, if it is longer than the pot itself. Here, the arrangement sits on the shelf of a white kitchen dresser that provides a stark contrast to the style of the design and makes the colours stand out even more.

The vivid red cockscomb (*Celosia* var. *cristata*) used as the object focuses the arrangement and helps balance the downward drop of the heavy pomegranates. The fillers are extra pieces of pomegranate blossom, bare branches and a second cockscomb, providing valuable elements of upward movement, giving height and balance to the whole design.

Standing the container next to a row of similarly shaped bottles strengthens its impact through repetition, while the sunlight on the container and the reflection of the plates is an unexpected bonus, as beautiful as it is vibrant.

Seasonal influences

Ikebana is a seasonal art form and, whenever possible, flowers that bloom at similar times of year are used together in arrangements. Using flowers in their natural season is considered a sign of respect for nature.

All of the arrangements covered in the section on techniques will change their character throughout the year. It's amazing how an arrangement made following the same basic instructions can look so different month by month.

In this chapter, each season is introduced by a haiku, a compact and evocative verse that goes straight to the heart of the subject and paints a vibrant word picture. With just a few flowers and branches, ikebana conjures up a powerful image in much the same way.

Birds are in blossom, trees begin to sing

And then it snows: the insanity of spring!

> HO-O

Spring

A basket with arum leaves and anemones

The anemones in this bamboo basket are tucked
under some arum leaves (*Arum maculatum*) for
protection, just as they might grow in the
garden. Anemones bloom in the spring in a
rainbow of colours, including red, blue, purple
and white flowers. The flowers can be single or
double with petals similar in shape to a poppy
and black poppy-like stamens. They grow on
long stems with deeply divided leaves, with a
pretty green 'ruff' just below the petals.

A kenzan hidden in the basket holds the
arrangement in place. The one used here is a
well kenzan that holds water, but it's just as
effective to use a small baked bean or salmon
tin to hold an ordinary kenzan. Just make sure
the tin has been thoroughly washed, then paint
it to match the basket.

A camellia flower

As it drops spills the water

From the yester-shower.

> BUSON

Camellia and buckthorn branches

The common name for the camellia is Chinese or Japanese rose. With their glossy dark green foliage and exquisite flowers they are an essential plant for the ikebana artist. There are many varieties used in both traditional work and free-style arrangements, as here. It is said that the skill of an ikebana artist can be measured by the way he or she handles camellias.

The camellia in this sculptural arrangement is the lovely 'Ave Maria', a cultivar of *Camellia japonica*. It flowers early in the year; contrasting it with heavy winter branches shows just how early. The branches are buckthorn (*Rhamnus cathartica*) collected from the wild coast of Cornwall and a strong container is needed to match their bold lines. The branches have been arranged as a frame for the single camellia bloom. No matter how you are using camellia flowers, never remove the top two leaves: the flower or bud should be framed first by its own leaves. Despite its fragility when set against the buckthorn boughs, the camellia is still the first thing you see in the arrangement – a good example of the power of beauty.

Spring landscape with peach blossom

This design is based on the upright moribana (see page 34) and uses three plant materials, peach blossom (*Prunus*), arum leaves (*Arum italicum* subsp. *italicum* 'Marmoratum') and 'Tete-a-tete' daffodils, plus driftwood. It is also a landscape arrangement (see page 101).

Peach blossom blooms very early in the spring and, as a symbol of femininity, is one of the traditional flowers used in Japan for the centuries-old Girls' Festival on the third day of the third month. On this day, arrangements are done in pink and yellow flowers. The yellow blooms are usually *nano-hana* (a member of the mustard family), while the pink ones can be peach or cherry blossom. Peach blossom should be used in as natural a way as possible and not bent or manipulated. The colour scheme of this landscape arrangement has been influenced by the yellow and pink shades of the Girls' Festival.

Diminutive 'Tete-a-tete' daffodils are dwarf hybrids with up to three small yellow flowers per stem. They are ideal for use in landscape work because you can use the whole plant – rather like a bonsai version of a full-size daffodil. In this arrangement the daffodils become the focus, acting as the object. The peach blossom forms the subject.

Arum leaves are used a great deal in ikebana in late winter and early spring. Versatile and easy to grow, they are some of the first large leaves to appear in the garden. In this species, they can be anything between 30-45cm (12-18in) long and have attractive white veins. Keep the leaves crisp by immersing in cold water when first cut until you need them.

This gentle early spring landscape holds the promise of warmer days to come and a wealth of flowers to follow.

Spring irises with willow

In ikebana irises are singled out for their poise, elegance and strength – qualities that are not so obvious when the flowers are massed together in bunches, as they so often are in Western arrangements. This arrangement captures the vitality of spring and the unique characteristics of the irises themselves. It is a visually exciting design, full of energy and movement. No matter which way you view it, it is equally impressive. In fact the thrill of this design comes from exploring how different it is from all angles.

Seven stems in a graduating design in the centre of the container have been used to illustrate the unfolding beauty of the flowers from tight bud to open flower. The arum leaves (*Arum maculatum*) at the bottom lend further weight and depth to the arrangement, giving it elegance and cohesion.

Willow is strongly associated with irises – both grow near water – and so the two plants are often used together in ikebana. Here the irises (*Iris* Xiphium Group) are framed by contorted willow (*Salix babylonica* var. *pekinensis* 'Tortuosa'), making the design balanced and comfortable to the eye. The meandering willow branches also contrast with the forceful energy of the irises and connect the arrangement to the garden just visible beyond.

Light pouring in from the window highlights both form and texture. When shape is of utmost interest as it is here, placing an arrangement directly in front of a window creates a strong silhouette.

This is a substantial design and the bowl was chosen to give the necessary width and dimension to support it. The small touch of green in the otherwise opaque white bowl subtly integrates the container with the arrangement. The white tablecloth throws the light back upwards through the dish and the arrangement itself, while the light pours through the container, adding to the fresh spring-like effect.

Tulips and contorted hazel in a blue glass bubble

Although the flowers in this arrangement look exotic and unfamiliar, they are in fact tulips given an ikebana treatment (see below). Tulips originated in Turkey and are thought to take their name from the tulbend or traditional turban worn by the Turks. These days they are more commonly associated with the bulb fields of Holland and are used by all ikebana artists right across the spectrum of styles.

Although tulips mix well with many different plant materials, they look particularly beautiful with bare branches, making them very popular for spring designs. In this arrangement the tulips have been combined with fantastically twisted stems of contorted hazel (*Corylus avellana* 'Contorta') in a way that looks a little like the upright nageire style (see page 46).

Tulips are often combined with flowering branches too. Different species of flowering branches are rarely used together in arrangements. Instead ikebana artists prefer to add cut flowers to branch material and tulips are prized for their ability to combine with peach and cherry blossom and flowering quince (*Chaenomeles japonica*).

You can use tulips just as they come or you can try this simple technique to turn out their petals and make them look quite different. Gently stroke each petal, starting at the base where it joins the stem and working outwards. This will cause it to reflex or turn back. The easiest way to do this is to hold the flower in two hands, using your thumbs to stroke the inner surface of the petal and your forefingers to provide support behind the petal.

Tulips do have a tendency to rearrange themselves, twisting or drooping after you've carefully completed a design. To avoid this happening, give the flowers a long drink in shallow water while they are still in their cellophane wrapping from the florist. This helps to keep their stems straight (see page 154). Tulips take up a lot of water, so be sure to top up the vase each day.

The container in this arrangement is a pale blue glass bubble shot with pink and etched with brown lines. The tulips echo the pink tones and the contorted hazel mimics the etched lines – a good example of matching plant materials to the container to great effect.

Hellebores enclosed in glass

Hellebores flower from late winter onwards, making them ideal for seasonal spring arrangements. The pale green flowers tinged with pink used in this design are an example of the Lenten rose (*Helleborus hybridus*, formerly known as *H. orientalis*), a very variable species that has produced many different varieties in colours ranging from dark purple through to white. Their leaves are composed of sharp, spear-shaped leaflets in clusters of three to seven. Hellebores are native to Europe and Asia, and are well-known garden plants.

This arrangement is done in a popular glass cube vase. The hellebores are held in place on a kenzan that has been hidden with fine white gravel, available from shops specialising in aquarium accessories. Before you begin the arrangement and especially before you add the gravel, it's a good idea to put a small piece of white muslin over the kenzan to protect the pins. It won't prevent you arranging the flowers but it will stop the gravel from getting stuck in between the pins and save hours of valuable time picking it out. When the arrangement has died, simply empty out the gravel and remove the muslin.

As well as concealing the kenzan, the gravel should also disguise the water line, so don't overfill the container. Keep the water level close to or below that of the gravel – you don't want to see two horizontal lines. Top it up carefully each day and the flowers will last at least a week. The gravel has also been heaped up at the base of the flowers for extra interest.

The vase looks like a block of ice with the flowers preserved inside – a reminder that spring can be cruel as well as beautiful.

Irises in a boat design

The iris is one of the most popular ikebana materials and has been used for centuries. Of the many species and varieties of iris, the Japanese have two particular favourites that they use for traditional work: the Japanese iris (*Iris ensata*) and the rabbit-ear iris (*I. laevigata*). Irises have a special place in the festivals of Japan. For the Boys' Festival, for example, on the fifth day of the fifth month, arrangements are done in blue irises to represent upright, tall, young men. The sharp leaves of the iris, which are likened to Japanese swords, are said to symbolize courage.

Here irises are used to depict sails in a traditional boat arrangement, known as an *oki-fune* or 'boat in the harbour'. You don't have to use a special ikebana boat container – a narrow shallow dish will do. In this design the sails are furled and the boat is at rest. Three irises form three main lines pointing to the sky. This is similar to the simple hana basic rising style (page 22), but with three upward lines instead of two. The two arum leaves (*Arum maculatum*) at the base act as fillers. Sometimes a long slender branch coming out of the arrangement is used to represent the anchor chain.

This arrangement uses Dutch iris (*Iris* Xiphium Group), the sort most commonly sold in florists. Sometimes the leaves of these irises can be a bit battered: before using them for an ikebana arrangement you should reshape them. Trim off any damaged edges and cut them back to the original pointed shape. This is important as it helps to maintain the natural look of the iris and it won't cause the leaves to brown or die for the duration of the arrangement.

There is a superstition attached to this arrangement. Boat designs used to be placed or hung high up so that the water in the container was not visible – seeing water in a boat is a bad omen. The superstition still persists and some boat containers have a lid to hide the water.

Stones and trees that meet

My eyes glare straight at me

In this glazing heat

> KYORAI

Summer

A basket with roses and acer leaves

In this basket a beautiful rose looks up to the sun
surrounded by the leaves of a lime green acer tree, in
a simple free-style arrangement. The rose is one of
the prime flowers of summer and an important
flower in ikebana. Like the iris, it has been used for
centuries in flower arranging. Every kind of rose –
from small delicate wild species to long-stemmed
formal flowers – has a place in ikebana, in both
traditional arrangements and free-style sculptural
work. Roses are easy to use with other plant
materials, especially pine and other green branches.
However, you can easily make an arrangement with
roses alone, without using any additional material, as
their foliage is particularly attractive. In fact, at every
stage of its life cycle – bud, open flower and hips –
the rose is one of the most versatile plant materials.

In Japan the rose is a symbol of peace and when
arranged with pine the two together symbolize
everlasting peace. The colour of the flower has an
additional meaning: the pink rose in this design
means beautiful girl, while a really deep pink bloom,
for example, stands for shyness.

Peony in a glass block

Known in Japan as the first flower among flowers, the peony has an important place not only in ikebana but also in Japanese culture. It was introduced from China, where it is equally revered as a noble flower. The peony plays a large role in oriental art in general and in particular in screen paintings of the Edo period.

Because of their dominant beauty, peonies are often arranged alone. The traditional way to use them is in a peony basket without any other plant material: the small shallow basket has a huge handle to frame the peony within. Although no other species are used in a peony basket, peony buds and seedheads can be included for variety. In arrangements where peonies are combined with other materials, these must be noble plants such as pine and wisteria, which are said to enhance the beauty of the peony.

There are two types of peony: herbaceous species and tree peonies. When the two are used together, the arrangement has the meaning of riches and honours.

The container for this modern free-style design is glass and easily available on the high street. Frosted glass marbles in the base of the container hold the peony stems in place. The peony is used with its own foliage – no other plant material has been added. One leaf submerged in the water hides the stems: the rest of the design sits above the top of the container.

In this lively place

the peony

most beautiful

> SOEN (CHIYO-NI)

Pieris with golden-leaved and red-leaved acer in a colour-blocked arrangement

Early summer brings a huge variety of foliage and flowering shrubs. Sharp greens and soft pinks meld together in nature at this time of the year and that mixture of colours has been transported to a special suiban for this arrangement. The shallow container comes from the island of Crete and the inside has a patterned turquoise glaze the colour of the Aegean.

The plant materials used here are pieris (*Pieris* 'Forest Flame'), plus golden- and red-leaved varieties of the Japanese maple (*Acer palmatum*).

The pieris is a showy garden shrub and its fresh young foliage each year is a strong shade of red that turns pink and cream in turn until it eventually goes green. It is lovely to use at every stage of growth, but especially when it is crowned with trails of small white flowers, just like lilies of the valley. The acer leaves pick up the colours of the ever-changing pieris.

This arrangement is loosely based on the moribana slanting style (see page 36), but with the colours 'blocked' or kept together in groups. The red acer and the dark pink pieris leaves are separated from the pale pink pieris by a band of lime green acer leaves. It is a very natural effect with the materials mimicking the way they grow in nature.

A summer breakfast table

One of the great pleasures of ikebana is being able to take materials from a much bigger bouquet or arrangement to create something new, personal and utterly charming. This delicate design for a breakfast table holds memories – and flowers – from a summer wedding that took place the day before.

The free-style design is based on the simple hana basic rising style (see page 22). The main difference is that more fillers have been added – the purple gypsophila – to give the design extra movement and lightness. The subject line is the white bridal gladioli (*Gladiolus* 'The Bride'), soaring upwards and leaning to the right. The object is the strong dark purple lisianthius (*Eustoma grandiflorum*), which is in balance with the height of the arrangement. The other fillers are the second gladiolus that supports the main line and extra lisianthius flowers tucked behind to strengthen the object.

The design was made in a little bowl found in the kitchen cupboard: it suits the informality of the breakfast table and adds a spontaneous feel to the arrangement. The delicate conical bowl has a slightly raised base that lends additional height and elegance. The lilac tablecloth and napkins tone perfectly with the flowers, creating a soft, relaxed effect.

Waxing moon arrangement with white clematis and golden acer

In the Far East there is a great deal of interest in the phases of the moon. Moon-viewing parties are held at certain times of year, especially for the full moon at harvest time and the hunter's moon in October.

In ikebana, moon arrangements capture the spiritual element of the art and emphasize the close relationship that the Japanese have with nature. Moon arrangements are done by all ikebana schools, with a different design for each of the three phases.

You do need a special moon container for these arrangements: a circular wooden container that is wider at the base than the top. The wood holds water and the flowers sit in the base.

The waxing or new moon arrangement has a long branch – about twice the diameter of the container – sweeping out to the left. This branch is like the subject line in the slanting moribana (see page 36). The object is a third of the length of the subject and is usually composed of flowers.

In the design for the full moon, all the material is contained within the circle of the moon container. It is made with an upright main line, and the flowers that form the object are placed at the base of this branch.

Finally the waning moon arrangement is like waxing moon but the long branch sweeps out to the right instead.

This waxing moon that appears to hang in space features the luminous white flowers of the clematis 'Valge Daam' and a long branch of golden-leaved acer. Its surreal quality is enhanced by suspending the container on a length of fishing line instead of a traditional bamboo pole so that it looks like a summer moon drifting across the sky.

Sculpture with driftwood and a single sunflower

The bold brash sunflower is a typical summer flower. Its Japanese name *himawari* means 'turning with the sun' and when grown as a crop, the flower's habit of following the sun is obvious, as the orientation of the whole field of flowers changes throughout the day.

Although sunflowers are grown all over the world and easy to obtain, they are a little temperamental, which makes their use in ikebana somewhat limited. Their stems are very thick and the huge flowerheads will soon droop unless treated with care. The stems need to be conditioned before you start work, either by singeing the cut ends or boiling them in salty water (page 154). Sunflowers often seem to last longer if all their leaves are removed first.

The really big flowerheads are used mainly in sculptural arrangements as demonstrated in this design. The small ones are used in more traditional arrangements. Take great care when mixing them with other types of flowers as they are extremely dominant. Try combining the seed heads with the flowers in bloom to bring the past and the present together in one arrangement. The seed heads are also used extensively in modern and free-style arrangements.

This arrangement is a free-style design using just one sunflower and a piece of driftwood set in a round, ball-shaped container. The heavy flowerhead is held in place by a kenzan in the base, while the driftwood is simply resting in the vase.

Summer landscape with iris and calla leaves, and a water lily

The water lily (*Nymphaea alba*) is the most striking material in this arrangement and is supported by iris and calla leaves, plus its own floating foliage. In ikebana water lilies are always used just as they grow naturally and nearly always in water arrangements. In their natural habitat the flowers open in the day and close at night and their Japanese name *suiren* means 'sleeping flower'.

Water lilies are rarely offered for sale for the simple reason that the flowers close soon after cutting and will not open again. When you are cutting them at home, one way round this is to dribble warm candle wax into the open flower, in a colour that matches the petals. The wax sets and prevents the water lily from closing, allowing it to be used in an arrangement.

This is a close-up landscape design (see page 101), calm and tranquil in restful green and white. It is based on the upright moribana arrangement (see page 34): the iris leaves form the subject line and the water lily the object. Calla leaves (*Zantedeschia aethiopica*) have been used as fillers. The water lily is positioned alone in stark simplicity, framed only by its own leaves, to accentuate its beauty. Fussy extra materials would only detract from its importance.

The shallow black dish was the perfect shape for this arrangement but it wasn't watertight. A layer of yacht varnish (readily available from DIY stores) will seal any porous surface, opening up the possibility of using all sorts of containers for ikebana. In summer arrangements it is usual to leave an expanse of water showing to make the viewer feel cool and refreshed.

O Leaves, ask the breeze

Which of you will scatter first

From the verdant trees.

> SOSEKI

Autumn

A basket with Japanese anemones and autumn foliage

This is a typical Japanese basket full of autumn materials: Japanese
anemones (*Anemone* x *hybrida*), miscanthus grass and azalea leaves.
You can almost smell the earthy scent of autumn and sense the
approaching winter.

Japanese anemones are some of the last flowers to come into
bloom in the garden. They have long, graceful stems and are used a
great deal in ikebana work, but need to be handled carefully or they will
droop if not properly conditioned (page 154). They should be cut
underwater and be given a good drink before arranging.

Miscanthus is a species of ornamental grass native to Japan. It is one
of the *aki-no-nana-kusa* or Seven Grasses of Autumn, a series of
species all chosen for their small flowers in muted shades that are ideal
for introducing a hint of autumn mist. Flowering stems of miscanthus
shrivel quickly: when using them in an arrangement, keep a few stems
in reserve and replace the flower heads regularly. For this design the
miscanthus leaves have been removed as they grow at right angles to
the stem and would have been too intrusive. But in other arrangements
they are often left in place to represent the wind blowing. Finally,
colourful azalea leaves add a typical hint of autumn.

Modern one-row style using cosmos and gayfeather

An asymmetrical arrangement with many upright lines is the essence of this modern linear design. The container is a long, low one and although it is a special ikebana design, you can just as easily use a long shallow trough.

The materials used here are gayfeather (*Liatris spicata*), cosmos (*Cosmos bipinnatus*) and small, young bergenia leaves. The upright purple gayfeather flowers at either end of the container are the subject and secondary lines and the shortest red cosmos looking straight out from the arrangement is the object. Glossy green bergenia leaves, extra cosmos and gayfeather all act as fillers.

Three kenzans hold the materials in place. Although it's tempting to use a whole row of kenzans to make the arrangement, you get the best results by spacing them out and leaving room for the 'breeze' to blow through.

Gayfeather is originally a North American species but is now indispensable in ikebana because of its long straight stems. Neither is cosmos a traditional Japanese species: it was imported in 1868 and has been used for ikebana ever since, especially in free-style work, as it grows with interesting twists to the stems. It is also valued for producing masses of autumn flowers in white and pink. In Japan white cosmos flowers have the emotional meanings of purity and elegance.

A heavenly design using phormium leaves, autumn leaves and late pink lilies

More conventional autumn colours are evident in this arrangement. The design is known as the heavenly style, so called because of the way the subject line rises straight up towards heaven. It is based on the simple hana basic rising style (page 22), but has added fillers in a third material. Leaves of the New Zealand flax (*Phormium tenax*) form the subject line; the object is a late flowering pink oriental lily and the fillers are small branches of autumn azalea leaves.

A brown suiban with a noticeable central notch in the base holds the arrangement. The kenzan has been placed so that it lines up with the notch, centring the arrangement in the container.

All the colours of the design are in harmony with each other. This variety of phormium has beautiful pink leaves striped with brown and green that tone with both the pink lily and the brown suiban. The azalea was chosen for its stunning deep pinky red leaves. It has been used in small branches as it breaks very easily and cannot be bent into shape like some other materials. It is best to use azaleas by studying the shape of the branch as well as leaf colour.

Nights are drawing in and winter is just around the corner. The ikebana artist is only too aware of the changing seasons and this arrangement is a farewell to summer.

Bringing autumn indoors

It is always satisfying to be able to create something so graceful from so few materials, especially branches that have been picked from the garden or gathered on an autumn walk. Here, found materials have been supplemented with just three gerbera flowers from the florist.

In this free-style arrangement, the main line is a tall spreading branch of viburnum with a few leaves left at the tips. Although most of its leaves have fallen, that's no reason to reject it: its near-leafless state is a way of indicating the autumn mood. The inclusion of dried fatsia leaves (*Fatsia japonica*) provides an interesting textural contrast to the gerberas and crab apples, plus a poignant reminder of the transience of all things. The driftwood provides further texture and anchors the arrangement visually, as well as disguising the kenzan.

The arrangement was deliberately placed to be the first thing you see when you enter the room. Bathed in sunlight that pours through the french doors, you are reminded of the way light filters through sparsely clad trees on a sunny autumn afternoon. The delicate lines of the stems and patterns of the leaves are highlighted to great effect. A large design like this benefits from being given a lot of space and an abundance of natural light so that you can appreciate the shapes of the branches and subtlety of the contrasting materials.

The large plastic dish that holds the arrangement is practically invisible, making the design the star attraction.

Morimono design with an orchid and autumn berries

The Chinese have a tradition of arranging fruit and vegetables on a rectangular board and this custom came to Japan in the form of *morimono*. Morimono means to place things on something. No vase is used and any materials can be combined, provided they are fresh and grow in China. (Morimono arrangements are part of Bunjin style, page 99)

There are no real rules for the arrangement. Guidelines are based on the moribana designs so that materials placed on the board are in the shape of a scalene triangle (see page 33).

Along with the fruit and vegetables, flowers may be arranged too, but the whole plant must be used. That means flowers, leaves and washed roots. In this example, an autumn-flowering orchid has been used in its entirety. This is a transitory art form and the orchid won't die. You can safely leave it for a week if you spray it with water daily. The orchid can be replanted at the end of the week with no ill effects. If you are worried about doing this with a prize or delicate specimen, choose a species that is epiphytic instead and grows naturally with aerial roots.

The other materials are a long branch of red hawthorn berries (*Crataegus monogyna*) and a few scattered cape gooseberries (*Physalis peruviana*) – small, edible golden fruits in papery seedcases.

The line of the arrangement – the scalene triangle – is marked by a beautiful piece of driftwood and the cape gooseberries. The materials are placed on a flat board, typically rectangular and lacquered in black as here. A large ceramic plate, a woven bamboo mat or even a banana leaf would also be suitable, but when choosing materials to display, always take the colour of the board or tray into consideration.

Combinations of materials should be sympathetic to each other. In autumn, fruit, vegetables and flowers are ideal, especially at harvest time.

Nageire style arrangement with an ornamental cabbage and a leek flower

There's not an autumn leaf in sight, yet this unusual arrangement has a very real sense of harvest time and the changing seasons

The design is based on the slanting nageire (see page 48) but achieves a completely different look by using vegetables for plant materials. The cabbage to the fore of the arrangement is the object and the leek flowerhead forms the subject line. A tall, slender slate-grey pot complements their colours and textures.

The cabbages (*Brassica oleracea*) are actually an ornamental variety specially grown as cut flowers – they are readily available and are often sold on very long stems. They are popular for sculptural ikebana work, as their big bold shape makes a good focus to an arrangement. These particular ornamental cabbages are dark green edged with purple and they have great appeal to the modern arranger. They also come in pale pink and white with frillier leaves (see page 145).

Ornamental onions or alliums are familiar cut flowers with smooth curving stems popular for modern arrangements. But the allium in this design is actually a leek gone to seed in the artist's garden. It grew with this extraordinary twist to the stem and was anxiously watched over until it was at a perfect point to use. This autumn arrangement is a good example of how you can use nature itself to produce unusual materials that add a real 'wow' factor to your work. By keeping an eye on what is growing around you, your designs will be so much more interesting.

The hills cast shadows,

And the pampas grass is swaying

In sunlit meadows.

> BUSON

Autumn landscape with acer foliage, hydrangeas, iris leaves and seedheads

An autumn landscape arrangement imitates the way the garden looks at this time of year: a little weather-beaten but with flashes of colour. As a general rule, landscape work uses three, five, seven or nine plant types.

The five materials used in this realistic design are acer branches with lichen and coloured leaves, red-berried cotoneaster, creamy white *Hydrangea paniculata* flowers, iris seedheads and leaves, and the brilliant yellow *Sternbergia lutea* flowers.

This arrangement was created using three kenzans and is loosely based on the moribana arrangements. The large dark blue suiban allows plenty of space for the plants.

In landscape designs as the seasons change, so the amount of water showing in the suiban varies. As winter approaches the amount of visible water is reduced so that when winter is well and truly here no water would be showing at all. The water is concealed by using a ground-cover plant material, which needn't count as one of the landscape materials. Various plants can serve as ground cover: here, club moss has been used to cover nearly half of the surface area. Other alternatives include parsley (for summer landscapes) and tiny bundles of yew needles painstakingly wired together then arranged to look like grass. Whichever ground cover you use, always keep it below the rim of the container.

Ikebana artists use plants as they appear in nature and this is especially true for the seasonal landscape arrangements, where including appropriate plants emphasizes the time of the year.

Willow trees are bare

Dried the water, and the stones

Lie scattered here and there.

> BUSON

Winter

A basket with pine, rowan berries and pampas grass

Pine, pampas grass (*Cortaderia selloana*) and rowan berries (*Sorbus aucuparia*) in a lacquered bamboo basket give a real feeling of winter. The soft feathery flowers of the pampas grass look like snow settling on the evergreen pine, while rowan berries make a flash of vivid colour, just as they do in the winter landscape. Pine, king of the trees, is one of the most traditional ikebana materials. It is often used in festival arrangements, especially at New Year. Pine symbolizes constancy, endurance and happiness, hence its importance at Japanese weddings.

Short-needle pine has been used for this arrangement. It is essential to clean the branches before arranging by removing all dead and broken needles, leaving the pine looking fresh. It is also a good idea to remove the leaves from flowers – or in this case berries – being used alongside, so that, as here, the pine is the only green in the arrangement. Pine has the ability to look good with almost any other plant material and this technique shows it at its best, without the distraction of other foliage.

Pampas grass is native to South America but generally grows well in gardens. In ikebana, it can be difficult to use and needs to be trimmed to avoid dominating any design. Here, only one small piece has been used, to help accentuate the orange of the rowan berries and the delicate green pine.

Buckthorn and bittersweet berries in a tall pot

This is a free-style arrangement based on the slanting nageire (page 48) but without a specific object. The sharp, bare buckthorn branches (*Rhamnus cathartica*) tell of short days and long cold nights. Long strands of red bittersweet berries (*Solanum dulcamara*) cascade down the container like drops of blood, just as they trail over a hedge in the garden. Although the berries are small, they make dramatic splashes of colour that immediately attract your attention. (Incidentally, the berries are poisonous – bittersweet is a member of the deadly nightshade family.)

The small piece of evergreen pine plays an important role by putting life into the design. The pine appears to be the only living green thing in the design, and its symbolism of enduring and everlasting life holds the promise that winter will end and the world will be green again in spring.

Using a tall, narrow pot in slate grey accentuates the height of the design and highlights the spare elegance of the branches. The branches were deliberately chosen to look like winter trees and they are vital in making this a winter arrangement. The pot is known as a mother pot because it is one of a pair – mother and daughter – the mother being the tallest. (The daughter pot of this pair has been used for the cabbage and leek arrangement on page 88.)

Twisted driftwood, arum leaves and a single oriental lily

The white oriental lily (*Lilium* 'Casa Blanca') has a glorious perfume and huge waxy flowers. Although in the garden it blooms in summer, as a cut flower it is available all year round and so can be used in a winter arrangement.

Lilies are notorious for producing highly visible pollen that stains their pristine petals – as well as clothing and soft furnishings. In a design using just one flower, it's important that it looks perfect, so for this arrangement the pollen-bearing anthers have been removed. All you need to do is pull them off with your fingers but leave the long filaments in place.

Arum leaves (*Arum maculatum*) are useful in winter when there is very little foliage available.

The weathering and lines on the twisted and bleached driftwood are repeated on the slate grey container, and the wood wraps around the pot and swings out to the side rather like the slanting nageire (page 48). Although this is, strictly speaking, a free-style arrangement, it shows how the balance and techniques learned in the fixed arrangements can be applied to free-style work.

A mass of fiery lilies

On a cold, wet winter day, the best place to be is sitting by the fire in a comfortable chair. The fireplace and imposing red chair form the focal point of this room. Linked to them in colour and shape is a mass of vibrant red lilies. These seem to crackle and spark like the flames of the fire behind, while the bold lines of bare azalea branches form a powerful contrast. The third material, dried fatsia leaves (*Fatsia japonica*), reflects the shape of the flames, while the grey-blue lichen on the branches alludes to the ash, after the fire has gone out. The rich tones of the flowers are reflected in the red velvet chair, while the black shallow dish and the dark wood of the table establish another strong visual link to the hearth. Placing the arrangement on a low table at the same level as the fire means it can be appreciated from a seated position anywhere in the room.

In this design you can see how effective the moribana style is in drawing out the unique qualities of the plant materials. The arrangement is based on the water-reflecting style (see page 38) and the wandering lines of old azalea branches covered with lichen conjure up the stark winter garden.

Filling the entire space with energy, the dynamism and movement of this arrangement extends well beyond its boundaries, successfully enhancing the room's cosy, convivial mood.

Bunjin-style design with pine and a phalaenopsis orchid

In essence, this winter arrangement follows the lines of the upright nageire design (page 46). But it is given an extra special touch by incorporating elements of a style known as Bunjin to transform it into a noble and spiritual arrangement.

Bunjin style affects the choice of material rather than actual arranging technique, and also attributes meanings to plants. Materials used must grow in China and have a Chinese influence. The style was developed during the late Edo period – when there was a cultural exchange between Japan and China – by the Chinese nobility who painted and studied art. Bunjin paintings from this era have a strong connection with ikebana and are worth investigating to learn more about this particular style.

Typically, Bunjin arrangements find beauty in twisted and gnarled wood: here a piece of driftwood has been used with a small branch of pine. Added to this is a complete phalaenopsis orchid, including root system. Phalaenopsis is considered a noble material and must be used with other noble species such as pine. Don't be tempted to add too many supporting materials that would spoil the orchid's impact.

Phalaenopsis or moth orchids bloom in winter and qualify as winter plant material, and orchids in general are considered typical Chinese flowers. To use the whole plant, lift it out of the pot and soak it in a bucket of water. Then hold the roots under running water to wash away the last traces of soil. The orchid can be repotted when the arrangement is finished and will grow on quite happily.

The arrangement has a natural appearance as the orchid appears to be growing out of the old wood. Rubber bands have been used to hold it in place, twisted round the base of the stems, behind the leaves and then on to the driftwood. The driftwood itself extends down into the tall Vietnamese pot for stability. Standing the whole arrangement on a polished black base is a traditional Bunjin touch.

Winter landscape using driftwood, hawthorn, sea holly and statice

Landscape arrangements are rather like paintings but use plant materials instead of paints to create a picture, using moribana-style techniques. They can be defined in several ways. The first and most obvious way is by the seasons they depict, then by plant materials used and finally by perspective.

Realistic landscapes use seasonal material in any combination to produce a natural-looking arrangement. Interpretive landscapes allow the artist to use any materials, not just plants, including stone and wood, to create a scene. The last category, traditional landscapes, uses only set plant materials and specific methods of arranging – it is too specialized to be covered in this book.

Perspective is just as important to an ikebana artist as it is to a watercolourist attempting to capture a landscape on paper, and much the same principles apply. Just as you would when planning a painting, it can be a useful exercise to practise framing a view with your hands or two L-shaped pieces of cardboard. In ikebana, landscape arrangements are divided into far distant, middle distant and near views.

This example is an interpretive landscape, which allows the artist a free choice of materials, and creates an impression of an estuary in winter. It is based on the water-reflecting moribana (see page 38) and uses seven materials: prickly sea holly (*Eryngium*), driftwood, pale purple statice (*Limonium sinuatum*), sea lavender (*L. platyphyllum*), dried scabious, berried hawthorn (*Crataegus monogyna*) and an ornamental grass.

Even in winter there is colour in the landscape as this arrangement illustrates.

Winter slanting nageire arrangement
with pine and protea

Bare trees and bushes are a never-ending source of shapes to be used in winter ikebana. These raw winter boughs of buckthorn (*Rhamnus cathartica*) immediately suggest harsh weather: you can almost feel the bitter wind whistling through the branches. The arrangement is based on the slanting nageire (see page 48). The buckthorn subject and secondary lines are easily recognised and the object is an imposing king protea flower (*Protea cynaroides*). A small branch of pine has been used as a filler. The arrangement also has a Bunjin influence (see page 99). The blue celadon pot is a typical Bunjin container with its crackle glaze and imitation handles, and is also standing on a Bunjin-style base. Traditionally the base would be a black lacquered board but here a slice through a rare elm burr has been used, buffed to a high shine.

Protea is very difficult to grow outside its native African habitat but is regularly imported as a cut flower. It is useful in winter arrangements: the jagged, divided bracts of the flower give it a spikey Jack Frost look. King protea can be used either fresh or dried – it's quite hard to tell the difference. The one in this arrangement is fresh but has had all its leaves removed. Intriguingly, the flower looks as if it has been frosted and gives a cold blue tinge to the picture.

This is a sharply sculpted winter design that will last for a long time

The blowing wind

    split, split by

winter trees

> CHIYO-NI

Ikebana at home

A floral art form like ikebana is invaluable for designers because of its ability to enhance the mood or structure of a space. An imaginative interior let down by unimaginative use of flowers is a missed opportunity. Flowers are often used as finishing touches to a room, but without some thought they can easily become 'lost'. With ikebana you are working directly with proportion, line, form, colour and space – a vocabulary shared with interior design – so you can choose an arrangement and position it in such a way that it has a direct relationship to the surrounding space. Flowers then become a focal point with impact.

There is a great feeling of space in this double aspect room, which was created by removing an internal partition wall, allowing natural light to enter from windows at both ends of the room.

Placed in the middle of the room, the arrangement is lit from all sides so its shapes textures, colours and three-dimensional quality are highlighted and displayed like a piece of sculpture. The arrangement stands out even further as it is loosely framed and contained by the rectangular space behind, providing a subtle contrast of linear and curved shapes.

The dramatic sweep of the cotoneaster branches are held in position by using a nageire-style fixing – a long stay that acts as a counterbalance (see page 45) – while the oncidium orchid bursts from the centre of the arrangement like a golden shower.

A sense of movement

The dramatic curving shape of green arum lilies (*Zantedeschia aethiopica* 'Green Goddess') suggested an arrangement based on the *hana-mai* design, which literally means 'dancing flowers'. And a kitchen dining table provides the opportunity for an arrangement designed to be viewed from all angles.

The lilies rise up from the container like two dancers and the leaves follow the lines of the lilies and join the dance. The trick is to establish a sense of movement and dynamic tension at the point where the two flowers almost meet, to create the focal point of the arrangement.

This design encourages you to walk round it. The arrangement is made possible by using a large shallow dish called a madoka – its legs add extra lift and elegance. Two kenzans are needed to make the most of the space. Using lilies facing in different directions gives a three-dimensional effect. The design is full of movement yet tranquil – a characteristic of ikebana. In addition, the space in the middle of the design is as beautiful as the flowers and draws attention to the feeling of light and space in the kitchen itself.

The vertical lines of the lilies against the horizontal shelves behind create another subtle pattern – an example of how surroundings can further enhance a design. You can even trace the curves of the lilies in the dining chairs.

From a line to a circle

A long kitchen table provides the right setting for an arrangement known as *hana-isho-narabu* or linear flower design. This example is just over 1m (3ft) long and is a three-dimensional one-row design meant to be seen from all sides, making it an ideal table arrangement (unlike the front-facing version on page 118). Each person has their own view of the flowers but without having to struggle to see other diners.

The soft colours and choice of materials – white chincherinchees (*Ornithogalum thyrsoides*), pale pink lisianthius (*Eustoma grandiflorum*), dark pink alstroemeria, cow parsley (*Anthriscus sylvestris*) and ming fern (*Asparagus umbellatus*) – create a fresh, informal feel, enhanced by the curve of the containers.

This kind of design draws our attention to the beauty of the materials themselves. It illustrates one of the main aims of ikebana: to draw out the unique character of the materials through placing them carefully, which in turn intensifies the mood the flowers are capable of expressing.

So often, only flowers in full bloom are considered for an arrangement. In ikebana, all stages of a plant's life cycle are valued. Here the inclusion of so many flowers in bud creates a sense of promise and optimism, and this kind of design would be a clever way of celebrating a child's birthday.

Varying the lengths of the stems gives a three-dimensional effect, while the use of several kenzans allows for a greater sense of movement and space.

These particular containers can be rearranged to form a circle – a *hana-isho-mawaru* design (mawaru means circular). But don't feel constrained by having to use special Japanese dishes. The designs can be made separately in ordinary narrow or circular dishes.

Harmony in repetition

In the West the fireplace is generally thought of as the focal point of a room, just as the tokonoma is in the East. Here the challenge was to create an arrangement for the mantelpiece to match the imposing style of the fireplace while using just a few elements for impact.

The simplest of all ikebana designs have been used, proving you don't need fancy ideas to get the desired result. The amaryllis (*Hippeastrum*) and contorted willow (*Salix babylonica* var. *pekinensis* 'Tortuosa') in the tall pot follow the simple hana rising style, but rather than using the diameter of the container as a guide to measuring the subject line, the height was used instead. The design in the low container is a variation of the simple hana slanting style. They are both two-line, two-material arrangements (see pages 22-31).

As in contemporary interior design, when you are using fewer materials, quality and form become even more important. The amaryllis was chosen for its size, colour and texture. It can certainly hold its own in a large space, while red against a white background will always look more intensely coloured.

Harmony is created between the designs and the elements in the room by repetition and by the way in which the eye follows the different heights and movement of the willow.

This is a great example of using a few materials to create an impact in a large space. Even though the designs are high up, the flowers face directly towards the viewer, creating immediacy and even intimacy in an imposing room.

Light and dark

The strong contrast between a heavy dark container and the dreamy softness of the white sofa and rug creates dramatic impact.

Initially placed to be seen at its best on entering the room, the arrangement also takes into consideration the fact that people will be seated at some point. It is low enough for people to still be able to see and talk to each other when sitting down. Notice how the shape of the vase echoes the curved legs of the table. The bare azalea branches take the eye up and to the side, and connect the arrangement with the surrounding space.

In a traditional Japanese setting, the lower line of the arrangement would have led your eye out to the garden. Here it leads instead to the sofa, the main focal point in the room. The azalea branches stand out in sharp relief against the soft white rugs and

upholstery: by contrast, their rough and gnarled texture makes the sofa look even more inviting.

Using a heavy container means choosing strong materials in terms of colour, line and form to avoid the vase dominating the arrangement. Here, the materials used are azalea branches with lichen, phalaenopsis orchids, bird of paradise (*Strelitzia*) leaves and pine. If you look closely you will see that the design is based on the slanting nageire (see page 48), with the azalea branches as subject and secondary lines and the orchid as the object. The bird of paradise leaves used in place of fillers are too dominant to actually play the part of true fillers. They give the design added weight and mass and turn it into a free-style arrangement. You can see why sculptural ikebana designs like this are best suited to interiors that are spacious and uncluttered.

Echoes of glamour

Ikebana is good training for anyone interested in interior design. It increases sensitivity to space and proportion, balance, colour and texture, which in turn influences how we see interiors. If you practise creating a design with fewer materials that makes positive use of space, it will give you more insight and courage to apply similar principles to interiors. It will give you the confidence to take away, to leave space around furniture: you will want to see shapes and lines more clearly.

The curvaceous lines of a French wrought-iron table were the starting point for this design. As it is very open and light, a heavy design would look out of place and overpower the delicacy of the table. Correspondingly delicate materials were chosen. Glory lilies (*Gloriosa superba*) that seem to float and dive in all directions are held in an Art-Deco style lacquered bamboo basket. (A water container hidden inside the basket keeps the plant materials fresh.) The work is given some depth by the fatsia leaves (*Fatsia japonica*) inserted at the back of the arrangement and reflected clearly in the mirror.

Every detail of this design, from the lustre on the lacquered basket to the lacy sprays of gypsophila, works in harmony to imbue the room with glamour and flamboyance.

Simple highlights

This simple design shows how ikebana can complement more highly decorative pieces like this elaborate antique Venetian mirror.

Tall curcumas and dahlias have been used in a heavenly-style arrangement, a variation on the simple hana rising style (see page 22). The tallest curcuma is the subject line and the foremost pale pink dahlia is the object, and the design has been positioned so that it is the first thing you see when you enter the room.

The curve of the bowl and the curves in the mirror are very similar, making it an easy transition for the eye to link the two elements together. The effect produced is one of tranquillity and stability, in contrast to the swirly shapes of the mirror.

It is an effective juxtaposition, brought to life by the shimmering reflection of trees and shrubs in the garden, connecting the design with both the interior and nature outside. Flowers, container and mirror are also united by the use of similar colours. The top of the tallest curcuma leads your eye upwards to the mirror, linking the two in yet another way.

Lining up

A narrow shelf won't comfortably allow for a standard vase, yet this bathroom ledge makes an ideal place to display flowers. The ikebana arrangement used was chosen precisely for its linear shape. The flowers are organised in one long line based on a design called a one row, which is a front-facing form of the three-dimensional design on page 108. Set in two 30cm (12in) rectangular containers, it is meant to be viewed from the front only and at eye level.

Four kenzans are needed as the flower materials are arranged at four points. Repetition is the key interior-design element here: there is plenty to look at as the eye travels along and up the arrangement.

The coloured glazes on the containers blend well with the plant materials, especially the pinky-brown, upright, striped leaves of New Zealand flax (*Phormium tenax*). The other materials are pin-cushion proteas (*Leucospermum*), autumnal viburnum leaves, fennel flowerheads and perfectly spherical yellow heads of craspedia.

The vertical lines of the plants echo the panelling above and below, contrasting with the overall horizontal span of the arrangement; the sprays of viburnum at each end take the reach of the design out even further.

Flowers positioned where you least expect them – for example, above the bath as here – create an extra element of pleasure in a room.

Setting a restful tone

The colours and textures in this opulent bedroom inspired the use of equally exotic flowers. The arrangement is based on the simple hana slanting style (see page 26), using purply-pink phalaenopsis orchids and pine, which are both noble plants held in high esteem in ikebana.

Notice how the spikes of the pine needles emphasizes the softness and delicacy of the orchid. Even a small piece of pine can scent a room, which is an added bonus.

The container is made from shell. Its gold lustre tones with the hint of gold in the wallpaper, while the slightly raised base gives the arrangement both extra height and presence.

In a bedroom, a design should harmonise with the surroundings to establish a restful, intimate tone. Small designs are better than large showy arrangements. Tall containers should also be avoided to keep things low key.

Arrangements should be designed so that they can be appreciated by the person in bed – for example, they should be displayed at a low level and should use flowers that create a gentle mood. Ikebana has the unique quality of being both restful and exciting at the same time

An exercise in restraint

With the ever-increasing popularity of interior design – just look at the number of TV programmes and home design magazines produced – we have much more understanding about how spaces work. Flowers, and ikebana in particular, can be used to enhance the mood, feeling or structure of a space to great effect.

Two hana arrangements have been used here in this sleek, streamlined contemporary kitchen. In this highly practical space, the mood is crisp and clean. The arrangements respond to this with strong lines and restrained use of materials. There are no long branches to get in the way or hamper the use of the worktops.

Using 'Green Woodpecker' gladioli and gerberas, the furthest arrangement obeys all the rules of the simple hana rising style (see page 22). The one in the foreground is a variation, with the kenzan moved to the left.

Silhouetted against the garden door and against the black floor, the strong vertical outlines of gladioli stand out and make a bold shape on their own. You don't often see them singly, or in lime green for that matter, but usually in bunches when their form is blurred. Could this be why we consider them a bit naff? Here, the emphasis on shape and repetition has an Eastern feel. The accent is not on the worth of the object but on its pleasing outline.

This design, simple though it is, is almost a feat of engineering. Men in particular are drawn to ikebana – perhaps this aspect of construction and angles attracts them?

Through precise measurement and placement, ikebana teaches you to see things in relation to each other; you soon become quick at making mental visual comparisons and measuring by eye.

Radiating style

You don't need a totally minimalist environment to display ikebana. Just clearing a corner of a room or table gives an arrangement space to breathe.

This arrangement is called a *hana-isho-hiraku* – hiraku meaning radial. It's a design that looks great – but very different – from all angles. This type of design can also be described as a contrasting style, as each side of the arrangement features different materials in varying lengths.

The materials used are glory lilies (*Gloriosa superba*), honeysuckle (*Lonicera*), roses, alstroemeria, hypericum berries and ming fern (*Asparagus umbellatus*), all springing from one central kenzan. The longest branch of honeysuckle on the right is the subject line, from which all the others are measured (see page 18). The secondary line, the glory lily is slightly shorter, and the line of roses forms the object. The central rose is the first to be inserted, followed by another bloom on each side. The subject and secondary lines are each supported by slightly shorter stems in the same material. Short lengths of fern tucked into the middle form a green base colour.

Colour is an important aspect of this design: different shades are grouped together. Tawny pink alstroemeria buds are clustered on one side of the roses and red-and-green hypericum berries on the other. In ikebana, using flowers in the colour of the berries' original blossom gives the best results, hence the use of yellow roses to partner the hypericum berries. Notice how glorious the colours look against the early autumn landscape beyond.

Simple lines

The beauty of the lotus – its flowers, leaves, buds and seed pods – has inspired artists for centuries. Venerated because of its association with Buddha, the lotus (*Nelumbo*) symbolizes purity in an impure world. It rises from the depths of the pond, perfect and unspoiled.

Here, lotus buds and leaves are arranged in a simple heavenly style, with the three main lines reaching to the sky. This design follows the lines of the simple hana rising style, chosen for its graceful, elegant quality. It accentuates perfectly the natural upward growth of the lotus stems. Notice how some of the leaves are placed so that the intricate patterns on the undersides can also be appreciated. You are subtly reminded of the beauty in every aspect of nature.

The gentle arrangement works successfully with its container and its position within the room. The shallow dish raised on a stem mirrors the delicacy and upward movement of the flowers, and echoes the shape of the leaves. The space below the dish and the Perspex table contribute to an atmosphere of quiet suspension and watery calm.

This contemporary living space and the lotus arrangement share the common principles of simplicity, a feeling of space and structure. The arrangement draws from the elegance of the room, from its simple lines, pale colours and natural sunlight.

Evoking a mood

Ikebana frequently incorporates bare branches and unusual pieces of wood for the contrast of texture and line with flowers and leaves.

Interiors without any natural elements can become static and lifeless. It is refreshing and inspiring to come across an organic shape in a room of right angles and straight lines.

This arrangement draws its inspiration from an unusual driftwood mirror. The ikebana design, in a simple white kitchen container, is an example of complete harmony of materials. The arrangement evokes a windy day by the seaside, suggested by the angle of the driftwood, the blue sea holly (*Eryngium planum*) and tiny sprays of sea lavender (*Limonium platyphyllum*).

Based on the water-reflecting style of moribana, the driftwood is the subject line, with the sea holly as object and sea lavender as fillers. The design demonstrates how powerful the moribana style of ikebana is at conveying mood and a sense of place, through the skilful composition of just a few materials.

Combining colour and line

To have any real impact against the bold black and white tiles in this bathroom, flowers and plant materials must have equally strong shapes and colours. Although the cyclamen flowers in the arrangement pictured opposite are relatively small, their pinky red tone has a luminous quality and when massed together as here, they have real oomph. The graphic shape of the bamboo (*Pseudosasa japonica*) gives this simple hana slanting arrangement a fresh breeziness and simplicity appropriate for a bathroom.

Displayed on a modern Perspex table, the arrangement has extra impact and focus as there is little to distract the eye. Shallow dish arrangements like this one highlight the character of the materials used and are especially useful in bathrooms where simplicity is key.

This design has extra charm in that the materials come from the garden and are arranged in a simple kitchen bowl. Cyclamen last a long time as cut flowers and a few of their shapely leaves grouped around the base hide the kenzan. Once again you can see how you can make original designs quickly, easily and inexpensively – and in keeping with your own interior style.

On a practical note, in a bathroom it is obvious that you should avoid arrangements that are too big and interfere with use of the room or compromise safety.

Small and compact, this arrangement on the right is designed to be seen from above, standing by the basin. Placed in a small Japanese teardrop container, the tulips have been cut very short – 5-10cm (2-4in) – and their heads packed together at different angles to create a riotous pattern of silky colour and shape. The front tulip has been opened (see page 63) and forms the focus of the design.

Bright orange holds its own with the wall tiles, while the little sprig of green fern adds an extra note of freshness and highlights the green streaks running through the tulips.

Extraordinary effects with ordinary objects

Bright colours and strong shapes are hallmarks of retro design and are used here in a genuine retro setting. This is an ideal opportunity to be adventurous, proving that ordinary objects like these stainless steel bowls can be used to dazzling effect when they are grouped and spotlighted with the same care as if they were valuable antiques.

A low design based on repetition of shape and colour was chosen, to avoid interrupting the view from kitchen to living room. The bowls are placed at an angle that naturally leads into the space beyond, in the way that an old master angled an object such as a knife in a still life, creating depth and drawing your attention deeper into the composition.

The smaller bowls contain pyracantha berries and baby pumpkins, respectively. The larger bowl has a kenzan on one side to hold the cockscombs (*Celosia argentea* var. *cristata*) in place; it is hidden under the flowers themselves. The textures of the velvety cockscombs and the smooth pumpkins make an interesting contrast, while the colours look even more vibrant against the more neutral tones of the living room beyond.

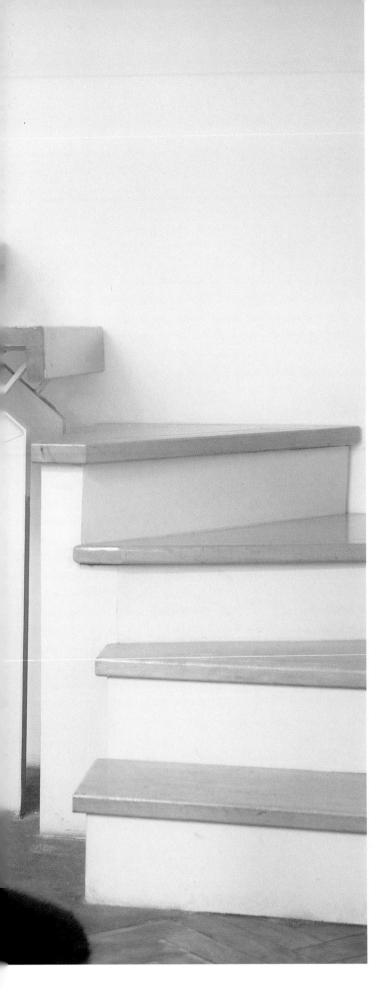

Matching bold with bold

When choosing a container, you need to consider not only colour, design and shape, but the overall character of the piece. Here a large angular area defined by the staircase is comfortably balanced by a bold curvaceous vase. A narrow light-coloured one would simply disappear in this space.

The weight and height of the container are strong enough to hold a large piece of weathered pine. A heavy arrangement like this must be made in situ – the pine is resting on the pot and is held in place with one of the fresh pine branches, pushed down into the container as a stay.

Five green chrysanthemums set in front provide a focus for the design. The beauty of the old pine wood is brought alive by the inclusion of fresh pine needles. Materials with a shared provenance work extremely well when placed together and you can see this to good effect with ikebana. The old and new pine materials make natural companions, creating an even stronger link with the world outside.

Additional visual links are formed between the arrangement and the dark rug and parquet floor. The angle of the ornamental grass mirrors that of the staircase and creates an impression of movement and height.

Seeing red

The inspiration for this design comes from the unusual mosaic glass tabletop. With a distinct character of its own, it presented a real challenge.

A funky glass container was chosen for its contrasting shape and colour, which, as you can see, reflects back as a pool of liquid red light. Containers in ikebana are much more than vessels for holding water. They are an integral part of the design. In fact, it could be said that in ikebana, flowers and their container are one.

To keep things simple and maximize impact, a red amaryllis (*Hippeastrum*) was chosen for strength of form and colour. Contorted willow branches (*Salix babylonica* var. *pekinensis* 'Tortuosa') create a relaxed, unconstrained sense of movement and contrast effectively with the flat evergreen cupressus foliage. They stretch outward into the space, integrating the arrangement with its surroundings.

Colour, light, mirrors and living objects are all great ways to enliven interiors. Another point to take into consideration is the fact that the table and design can be seen from a mezzanine level above. A vertical design wouldn't have nearly as much impact as the strong outline created by a more horizontal composition highlighted by the glass tabletop.

A study in colour

Light-hearted and fun, the geometric shapes, bold colours and materials of this flexible study/dining area played a big part in determining the choice of flowers and design.

Gerberas were selected for their strong colour and simple daisy-like shape. Their hot fuchsia-pink petals jump out at you; delicate pale flowers would be overpowered in this space. Gerberas have hairy stems that don't like standing in deep water, but in an open shallow dish the air can circulate around them and the flowers will last a lot longer. The soft feathery texture of the petals makes a contrast to the smooth, moulded plastic chairs and wall light. The round bowl and round flowers also balance the blocks of colour formed by the table, chairs and light.

The design is front facing and asymmetrical, the contorted hazel (*Corylus avellana* 'Contorta') reaching forward in different lengths. You can see here how the feeling of space and freedom from clutter calls for simple, well-executed flower designs – an important reason why ikebana is so useful to us today.

Natural elegance

The imperfect in nature has long been valued by the Japanese. This unusual sculptural piece of wood comes from Indonesia, where trees infected by a certain parasite become deformed into mushroom-like shapes as they grow. The mood of this simple, quiet room with its white floorboards and Indian-style day bed, influenced the choice of materials and style of this design.

With their strong, elegant arching shapes, arum lilies (*Zantedeschia aethiopica*) can look formal but here they appear very natural, cut to different lengths and placed pointing upwards just as they grow. The addition of a few large anthurium leaves reaching out in different directions enhances the movement and three-dimensional quality of the arrangement.

Lilies and leaves almost seem to float against the eau de nil colour of the walls. Light in tone but with lots of pigment, the colour has a fluid feel, enhancing the contemplative mood of room and arrangement.

A design like this is best created in situ. As well as being difficult to move when finished, it also means you can effectively assess the dimensions of the stand, container and flowers as you bring the whole arrangement together.

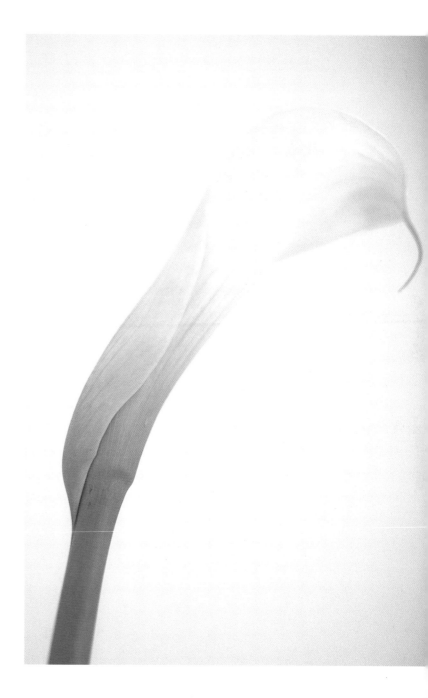

Contrasting shapes

The moon in all its phases is close to the heart of the Japanese. It features frequently in poetry, while moon-viewing is a custom that has endured for many centuries.

Flowers have always accompanied moon festivals, with some of the most interesting designs made using moon-shaped containers. These can hang from a stand, be suspended from a wire on the ceiling or stand alone, perhaps on their own plinth.

The different phases of the moon are represented by different arrangements (see page 74). Here two 'moons' of different sizes have been arranged in full-moon style with all the material confined within the container. In the larger moon, the upright bird of paradise stem (*Strelitzia*) is the subject line; in the smaller container, it is the bare azalea branch. In both moons, the object is the daisy-like gerbera flower facing forward towards the viewer.

The mantelpiece is narrow but easily accommodates the slender moon shapes. The circular containers and gerbera flowers are counterbalanced by the straight lines of the fireplace and rectangular log basket within. Using strong colour, contrasting geometric shapes and the principles of repetition and balance, your attention is drawn to the composition as a whole. The neutral black and white palette provides an effective background for the warmth and brilliance of the orange and yellows of the flowers.

A hint of autumn

This study area looks like a beach hut with its panelled walls and white floors.

The arrangement chosen to decorate it is a *rimpa*-style design that has its origin in the Ohara School of ikebana. It is based on the work of famous Edo screen painters such as Korin, Sotatsu and Hoitsu, who depicted natural scenes based on the seasons. In an intriguing reversal of roles, ikebana artists like to take their inspiration from the screen paintings and recreate them in real plant materials.

The arrangement uses fan shapes to make a bold pattern repeated across the two dishes. Rimpa designs usually give an indication of the season; here, autumn is conveyed by the seven materials used: creamy ornamental cabbages (*Brassica*) with encircling green margins, white pompom chrysanthemums, rose hips, grasses (*Pennisetum*), pine, acer and ming fern (*Asparagus umbellatus*). While the flowering grasses are used like an artist's soft brush strokes to add movement, they also echo the porcelain sculpture on the wall.

Rimpa-style designs occasionally include flowers more typical of a different season to mimic the unpredictability of nature – just as you sometimes find a rose blooming in the garden at Christmas or an unexpected primrose in autumn.

The arrangement is designed to be viewed from the front and can be kept close to the wall to allow plenty of workspace when the study is in use.

Reflected drama

The glamour of the Venetian mirror and the luxury of a large walk-in dressing-room formed the starting point for this arrangement. The sinuous curve of the glass vase is echoed in the curves of the calla lilies (*Zantedeschia aethiopica*), creating an immediate impression of elegance and femininity.

The arrangement began with the steel grass, which was tied in small bunches and gently persuaded into a half fan at the back of the vase, tall in the centre and sweeping out to the side. Then the stems of the three shorter calla lilies were bound together with covered wire, which holds soft stems without cutting into them. The wire is lower than the rim of the container to conceal it – binding the stems low also gives the arrangement a looser look. Finally, two taller lilies were added, one towards the back and one reaching out to the side. A single piece of wide-leaved bamboo used at the base gives the arrangement extra depth.

The height of the grasses leads your eye upwards and links the design to the mirror, creating a cohesive whole. The rich colour combination of vase and flowers, and the distorted reflection at the side of the mirror adds to the drama and beauty of this design.

Cool and effective

In this sparse modern bathroom, there is plenty of space for a tall pot arrangement to stand on the floor without getting in the way.

The style of arrangement is loosely based on the slanting nageire (see page 48) and the hydrangea and bamboo (*Pseudosasa japonica*) were both picked from the garden.

As ikebana involves using fewer materials, it is even more important to try to use plants that are strikingly coloured, unusually shaped and that contrast in some way. Here, the graphic shape of the bamboo provides an exciting contrast with the heavy round hydrangea heads; the clever juxtaposition of two very different materials brings out the best in each. The blues of the pot and hydrangea are cool and fresh – ideal for a bathroom.

You can almost feel the wind blowing through the bamboo leaves, while the bent steel grass is suggestive of rain. You can easily fold it back until it kinks to achieve this effect. As it stands, the arrangement has been designed and placed so that it can be seen as you come up the stairs and pass by on the landing. In this way it is appreciated by everyone walking through the house.

Introducing curves

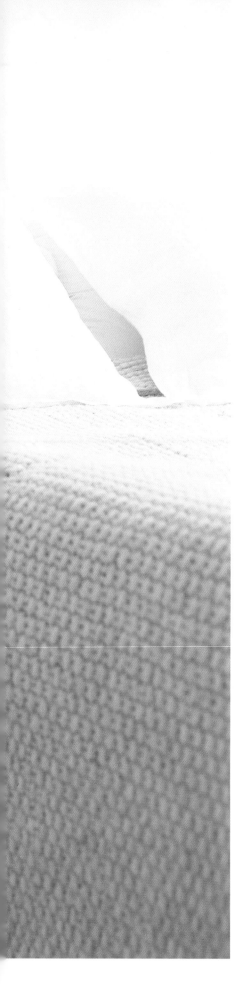

Many bedrooms are full of parallel lines –
think of beds, cupboards, tables and
windows. Adding some rounded, curved
shapes creates softness and balance.

Inspired by the quality of light,
coupled with the textures in the room, a
shallow stone bowl was used to create
an asymmetrical arrangement with
contorted hazel (*Corylus avellana*
'Tortuosa') on one side and five parrot
tulips on the other. Notice how clearly
the meandering lines of the hazel stand
out in this light, white space,
contrasting with the motionless upright
tulips. Soon the tulips will open, but if
you condition them before use (see
page 154), they will not droop so much
and, of course, will last much longer.

Tulips look particularly good with
bare branches like contorted hazel and
they are often used together in ikebana
(see page 63). Bare branches imply
weathered nature and time passing,
flowers are fresh and of the moment –
it's a great contrast. (Incidentally, bare
branches store well; you can use them
over and over again.)

The steamed bentwood stool and
the space it encloses add extra lightness
and delicacy to the design while the
stone bowl complements the texture
and colour of the cable knit throw.

Basic equipment

The basic equipment for ikebana is simple. Some of the tools shown here are imported from Japan, but it is easy to substitute. For example, Japanese shears or hasami have been specially designed to cut through stems in a range of thicknesses, but there is no reason why you shouldn't improvise with secateurs and scissors.

Probably the most important item of any arrangement in a shallow dish is the kenzan or pin-holder. You can buy pin-holders from most florists, though it has to be said that Japanese versions are better. Finally, there's nothing hi-tech about a bundle of sticks to make stays to keep plant material in place

Kenzans

Pictured below are three examples of kenzans – a round one and two triangular shaped. The latter are also known as ginkgo kenzans because their shape resembles the individual leaflets of the ginkgo tree (*Ginkgo biloba*). All kenzans have to be extremely heavy to balance the weight of different plant materials. The pins are sharp and close together to keep stems firmly in place. (See page 160 for stockists.)

Materials for making stays

These freshly cut sticks pictured above are used to make fixing stays for heavy branches used in tall containers, in both nageire and free-style arrangements. Green sticks are full of sap, which makes them springy enough to close tightly around the branch to be held in position. They will also bend before they snap, making them ideal to form the cross pieces used in tall pots. Tied in a bundle, they will keep for around 10 days before they lose their flexibility.

Basic tools

The tools pictured top right are as follows. Starting from the left, the syringe pump has two functions. It can be used to force water into the stems of plants such as water lilies and lotus flowers, as part of a conditioning technique (see page 154). Or it can be used to produce a fine water spray to mist plants with, both during preparation and after they have been arranged.

Next to the pump are two different pairs of hasami or shears; those on the left are stronger and can cut a larger range of plant material.

Beside the hasami is a pair of wire cutters to cut lengths

from the reel of fine florist's wire at the top. Wire can be useful for making fixings extra secure in nageire arrangements. (To bind soft-stemmed flowers or leaves together, it's best to use covered wire that won't damage the stems.) Never use hasami, secateurs or scissors to cut wire of any type – it will ruin the blades. On the far right is a handy folding Japanese saw for cutting thick branches.

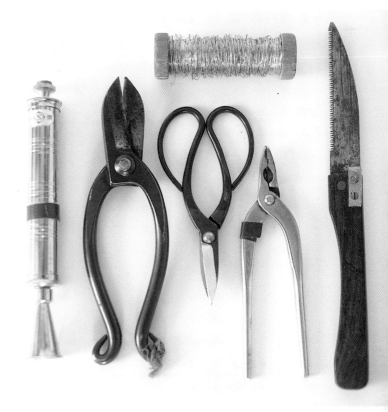

Containers

The selection pictured below will give you an idea. You need shallow dishes for simple hana and moribana designs – the small round bowl and the half-moon shaped one are ideal for simple hana designs, while the shallow oval container would be used for moribana.

For nageire you need tall pots. The pot on the right is an authentic Japanese design; the other is a typical department store vase.

Conditioning plant material

Cut flowers will last much longer if you treat them carefully. Over the centuries the Japanese have formulated a number of methods of conditioning cut flowers to ensure the longest lasting results possible.

Flowers keep their freshness by absorbing water upward through their stems. Whether picked or bought, all flowers benefit from a long drink in a bucket of deep water, for at least a few hours, but ideally overnight. The depth of water is important because it helps the stems draw in water by increasing the pressure on them. A few species – tulips, calla or arum lilies and gerberas, for example – should not be left in deep water and these are clearly indicated in the list that starts on the opposite page.

Although there are some chemical-based conditioning techniques, in general the methods described below produce good results for all ikebana plant materials.

Making a slanting cut underwater to increase water uptake

Mizugiri

All conditioning techniques have been developed to improve the rate at which cut flowers take up water. The most important technique is mizugiri, which describes the process of cutting of stems under water to prevent air locks from occurring.

Work in a bowl, bucket or sink with a reasonable depth of water and hold the stem underwater. Using hasami (or ordinary scissors or secateurs), cut off around 2cm (just under an inch) from the base of the stem. Make the cut at an oblique angle to increase the available surface area for the stem to take up water. Even if you know that you need to make a straight cut to arrange the flowers on a kenzan, you should still make the mizugiri cut at an angle and trim the stem again just before you start work.

If you are cutting a particularly delicate species from the garden, take a bucket of cold water with you and perform the mizugiri technique as soon as you've cut your material.

Yuage

Wrap flowers in damp newspaper or a damp cloth so that they don't suffer steam damage, leaving around 5cm (2in) of the stem exposed. Then place the ends of the stems in boiling water for about half a minute. Dip them into cold water immediately afterwards. Boiling water drives the air out of the stem, while the cold water forces the stem to contract and suck up water.

Yaku

Wrap flowers in damp newspaper or a damp cloth to prevent them scorching accidentally, leaving around 5cm (2in) of the stem showing. Char stem ends in a naked flame for half a minute until the surface is black. Most ikebana practitioners find a small camping gas stove useful for this technique. The heat gets rid of air in the stem and when placed in water, it will absorb the water to replace the air. It also sterilises the base of the stem, making it harder for bacteria to attack. Recommended for roses and some wildflowers.

Tsubusu

Tough stem ends can be crushed, without pulverizing them, to increase the surface area for water absorption. Or simply cut the base of the stem in a cross shape. This technique is recommended for woody plants such as pine.

Shio

Rubbing salt in some stems directly after mizugiri can improve water uptake through the process of osmosis. Shio is recommended for flowers such as calla or arum lilies, cockscombs and wildflowers.

Conditioning by flower type

Below are some suggested techniques for extending the life of plant materials featured in the book, plus tips for other popular cut flowers. Plants are listed alphabetically by their common name where possible.

Where alcohol is mentioned, this can be ordinary household gin, vodka or, if you want to be truly authentic, sake. Alcohol and vinegar both stimulate cut stems to absorb water.

acer younger growth is very difficult to keep fresh; where possible choose more mature foliage. Pick in the early morning, use yaku technique, then submerge branches completely in cold water, ideally overnight. Once arranged, a spray with cold water each day will be a big help.

agapanthus mizugiri if they begin to droop, then dip cut ends in alcohol or rub with salt.

allium no special treatment needed.

alstroemeria mizugiri

amaryllis (*Hippeastrum*) mizugiri

anemone mizugiri

anthurium mizugiri

aspidistra mizugiri; if the stems begin to bend, rub with salt and stand in water. When firm, cut again in fresh water.

azalea mizugiri

bamboo (many genera) pick very early in the morning. Put ends into boiling water and salt for a few minutes and then plunge into cold water.

bells of Ireland (*Molucella laevis*) mizugiri

bird of paradise (*Strelitzia*) mizugiri

black-eyed susan (*Rudbeckia*) mizugiri. If flowers begin to droop, try yuage.

bittersweet berries (*Solanum dulcamara*) mizugiri or, if drying the berries, spray with artist's lacquer.

branches with berries (most species) split stem end under water and peel back bark.

branches with leaves (most species) benefit from total submersion in water as moisture is taken in through the leaves.

broom (*Cytisus*) yaku and then submerge whole branch in cold water.

calla or arum lily (*Zantedeschia aethiopica*) Rub salt into end of stem and leave until it turns black. Then cut off the black part and stand cut stems in shallow water (deep water makes the stems split).

camellia mizugiri

carnation (*Dianthus*) mizugiri

cascading silver pear (*Pyrus salicifolia*) split branch ends underwater.

cherry blossom (*Prunus*) for all blossom, split the ends of the branch to about 2.5cm (1in), scrape some of the hard layers of bark away and place the branches in deep warm water up to the first flowers. Leave overnight before arranging.

chincherinchee (*Ornithogalum thyrsoides*) mizugiri

Christmas rose (*Helleborus niger*) yaku, then leave in cold water overnight, keeping flowers above water. Treat other hellebores in the same way.

chrysanthemum break stem ends underwater using your fingers – they absorb more water that way. If they persist in wilting, break again in cold water, followed by yuage.

clematis crush stems before placing in cold water. If flowers still droop, recut, then yaku.

cockscomb (*Celosia*) Try yuage or shio, then hold upside down and mist with water before arranging.

contorted hazel (*Corylus avellana* 'Tortuosa') mizugiri if in leaf; bare branches need no treatment.

cosmos after mizugiri, steep in hot salty water for a few minutes before arranging.

cow parsley (*Anthriscus sylvestris*) mizugiri, then leave overnight in cold water.

craspedia mizugiri

curcuma mizugiri

cyclamen mizugiri, then dip in alcohol for a few minutes. Or cut off flowers from a pot plant and arrange immediately.

cymbidium orchid mizugiri

daffodil and narcissi cut off the white ends: water is only taken up from the green part of the stem.

dahlia mizugiri, then dip in boiling salty water

delphinium mizugiri then stand in deep water for at least 15 minutes.

fatsia leaves (*Fatsia japonica*) mizugiri

Azalea leaves in autumn

Iris leaves and seed heads

fennel (*Foeniculum vulgare*) mizugiri, then dip stem ends in boiling water.

ferns (in general) mizugiri

flowering quince or japonica (*Chaenomeles japonica*) mizugiri

forsythia no special treatment required.

fox-tail lily (*Eremurus*) mizugiri

gayfeather (*Liatris spicata*) mizugiri

hardy geranium mizugiri, then singe the ends of the stems before placing in plenty of water.

gerbera mizugiri, then keep stems in shallow water.

ginger lily (*Heliconia*) mizugiri

gladiolus mizugiri

glory lily (*Gloriosa superba*) mizugiri

gypsophila mizugiri

hibiscus mizugiri but split stem ends underwater after cutting.

holly (*Ilex*) mizugiri but split stem ends underwater after cutting.

honeysuckle (*Lonicera*) mizugiri

hosta leaves submerge in cold water overnight.

hydrangea after mizugiri, slit or char cut end and leave in water for a few hours before arranging.

hypericum with berries split cut end or yaku.

iris mizugiri

Japanese anemone (*Anemone x hybrida*) mizugiri

jasmine (*Jasminum officinale*) mizugiri but ends may need splitting after they have been cut.

kerria (*Kerria japonica*) mizugiri

lisianthius (*Eustoma grandiflorum*) mizugiri

lotus (*Nelumbo*) cut stems then gently turn upside down and inject stems with water using a special pump. Put your finger

over the end of the stem, invert and put flowers into a bucket for a good four-hour drink. Cut them underwater again before you arrange them.

magnolia yaku until stems charred black, immediately after cutting; leave in water for a few hours before arranging.

mahonia no special treatment necessary.

marigold (*Calendula officinalis*) mizugiri

mimosa (*Acacia dealbata*) Split or crush the stem ends.

miscanthus and grasses in general boil cut ends briefly in vinegar to stimulate stems to take up water and then immerse in cold water.

monstera leaves mizugiri

New Zealand flax (*Phormium tenax*) mizugiri then stand in warm water and leave overnight.

oriental lily (*Lilium*) mizugiri but with a sharp knife rather than scissors.

pampas grass (*Cortaderia selloana*) mizugiri

peony (*Paeonia*) mizugiri then yaku or yuage. Keep immersed in deep water until needed, with flowers above water.

pieris mizugiri

pine mizugiri

poinsettia singe end or dip in alcohol and immerse in plenty of water.

poppy (*Papaver*) crush stem and steep in alcohol then immerse in deep water.

protea no treatment necessary.

pussy willow (*Salix*) no treatment necessary.

rhododendron mizugiri

rose mizugiri followed by yaku.

sea holly (*Eryngium maritimum*) no treatment necessary.

sea lavender (*Limonium platyphyllum*) no treatment necessary.

snowdrops (*Galanthus nivalis*) mizugiri

statice (*Limonium sinuatum*) no treatment necessary.

sunflower (*Helianthus annuus*) take a bucket of water into the garden when cutting sunflowers. Before placing in deep water, gently turn them upside down and fill the hollow stems with water. Put your finger over the end, invert and put them into a bucket for a long drink. Cut underwater again before arranging. Or boil the cut end in salty water.

Sternbergia lutea mizugiri

tulips mizugiri, then wrap in damp newspaper (or keep in their original wrapper) and leave in no more than 5cm (2in) water overnight to keep stems straight.

water lily (*Nymphaea*) inject vinegar into the stem using a special water pump, to stimulate stem tissue to take up water. For tip on keeping flowers open, see page 79.

willow (*Salix*) after cutting under water, strip off bark from end of stem or crush.

viburnum mizugiri, then crush stem ends.

wisteria mizugiri, then soak cut end in alcohol.

yew (*Taxus baccata*) no treatment necessary.

Glossary of Japanese terms

Vowels marked with a short line above are pronounced with a long sound. Where a word ends with an 'e', the 'e' should be pronounced.

aki-no-nana-kusa Seven Grasses of Autumn

Bunjin an arrangement with a Chinese influence

chabana flower arrangement for the tea ceremony

dō way, path of personal development, philosophy

dōbōshū priest/arbiter of taste

fuku secondary line in an arrangement

ginkgo triangular kenzan or pin-holder, taking its name from the gingko tree

go-shintai abode of deities

gyakugatte arrangement made on the right-hand side of the container

gyō semi formal

haiku a brief poem that encourages the reader to use their imagination to develop the idea further

hana flower

hana ishō flower designs

han-ishō-narabu linear flower design

han-ishō-hiraku radial flower design

han-ishō-mawaru circular flower design

hana-mai dancing flowers

hana-no-kokoro flower heart

hasami sharp shears used for cutting branches and flowers

heika tall pot for nageire arrangements

himawari sunflower

hongatte arrangement made on the left hand side of the container

ikebana the art of flower arrangement; making flowers come alive

Ikenobō one of the oldest schools of ikebana

kenzan sword mountain; pin-holder for plant material

kuge floral offerings for Buddha

kyaku guest; the object in an arrangement

madoka container with four small legs

mizugiri cutting stems under water to prevent air locks

moribana piled up flowers; arrangements made in a shallow dish

morimono design with a Chinese influence, made without a vase

nageire tossed in a pot; arrangement made in a tall pot

nano-hana yellow mustard-type flowers for the Girls' Festival

Nō Japanese theatre

Ohara school of ikebana founded by Unshin Ohara

oki fune boat at anchor; design made in a boat-shaped container

rikka standing flowers; ancient classical arrangement

rimpa arrangement inspired by screen paintings

seika simplified classical arrangement

shin formal

Shintō indigenous nature-worship religion of Japan

shio a conditioning method using salt

shohinka a shallow semi-circular container with a raised foot

shū master; subject line in an arrangement

sō informal

Sōgetsu an ikebana school founded by Sofu Teshigahara

suiban a shallow container

suiren sleeping flower; water lily

tokonoma display alcove in a traditional Japanese room

tsubusu a conditioning method that involves crushing the stems

yuage a conditioning method using boiling water

yaku a conditioning method that involves burning the ends of stems

A chabana-style arrangement

Index

Authors' acknowledgements

Diane Norman would like to thank:

Hilde Woodman, Sub Grand Master of the Ohara School, who was a wonderful teacher and friend, generous with her knowledge and a great inspiration to all her students. She died in September 1999 but was very encouraging in the concept of this book. Her husband John has lent valuable reference books and allowed his garden to be raided for plant material for photography – many thanks, John, for your help.

My husband Michael Norman, who has been a tower of strength, from shifting containers and crates of flowers to unfailing moral support

The editorial photography and design team – Verity Welstead, Sue Storey, Miranda Swallow – and Sharon Amos for being such a patient editor. It's been terrific working with all of you.

Dr Nicola Beck for the use of her apartment for photography; Elizabeth Nation, Sogetsu and Ikenobo Master, for all her help; Rachel, head gardener at Exbury Gardens in Hampshire (02380 891203), for providing branches and flowers for photography; Jane, Gary and Lisa at Courtesy Flowers in Bournemouth (01202 300444); Stephen and Mark at Bloomsbury Flowers in London (020 7242 2840) and photographer Dudley Button.

Finally, I'd like to thank Michelle my co-author.

All arrangements photographed in this book were created by Diane Norman. You can visit her website on www.ikebanaandwatercolours.com.

Michelle Cornell would like to thank:

Lorraine Dickey for her vision and for taking the plunge in commissioning this book, and everyone at Conran Octopus who helped pull it together with such professionalism and panache. It was a real team effort. A special thanks to our editor, Sharon Amos whose calm, thoughtful approach inspired the confidence and good feelings so necessary in meeting the challenges of writing.

Senei Ikenobo, present Headmaster of the Ikenobo school for providing me with an invaluable reference point and an example of a true Japanese ikebana master. Gas Kimishima for sharing his knowledge with me so generously and encouraging me to find my own way with simple flowers, and my co-author Di.

Afra Cambridge for her friendship and positive encouragement, and Maxine Holden for sowing the seeds of my love of flowers and for sharing her garden with me over the years. Also a special thanks to Georgina Cornell, for her enthusiastic appreciation of my own ikebana, and to Richard Gallehawk of The Dorset Water Lily Company (01935 891668), for supplying us with wonderful lotus plants at short notice.

Finally, most of all I'd like to thank my dear partner, Michael Breen, whose constant support and help with my research and thinking made it possible for me to get the job done.

Email ikebana@dircon.co.uk for details of Michelle Cornell's London-based workshops.

Publisher's acknowledgements

The publisher would like to thank the following photographers, galleries and agencies for their kind permission to reproduce the following photographs in this book:
Page 9 Mary Evans Picture Library (Artist: Hokusai);
10 Paul Quayle/Axiom Photographic Agency; 11 Mirei Shigemori Collection (Artist: Fushun-Ken Senkei); 12 Mirei Shigemori Collection (Artist: Hosokawa Tadaoki Sansai); 13 Tokyo National Museum (Artist: Suzuki Harunobu c.1765); 14 The Asiatic Society of Japan – Illustration to a reading by Josiah Conder on 13 March 1889.
Pages 58-59, 70-71, 94-95 Dudley Button.

Every effort has been made to trace the copyright holders, artists and designers and we apologise in advance for any unintentional omissions and would be pleased to insert the appropriate acknowledgement in any subsequent publication.

Page 151 steamed bentwood stool by Glyn Bridgewater; page 145 porcelain wall hanging by Jo Whiting and wishbone chair by Hans J Wegner; all courtesy of Parma Lilac (020 8960 9239).
Page 129 driftwood mirror from Sea (0208 340 1000).
Pages 98, 104 and 134, vases courtesy of Jacqueline Edge (020 7229 1172) www.jacquelineedge.com.

Where to find equipment
Some ikebana equipment can be bought mail order. Try visiting the website for German stockists Fuji Hana at www.ikebana-fuji-hana.com or the Ohara School website on www.ohararyu.or.jp/english/catalog/index